MORE YARNS ON CHRISTIAN PIONEERS

BY

ERNEST H. HAYES

Author of
'The Pioneer Series,' 'The Child
in the Midst,' etc. Founder and
Editor of 'The Concise Guides.'

THE RELIGIOUS EDUCATION PRESS, LTD.
WALLINGTON   **SURREY**

1953

First printed	.	.	.		1933
Second impression	.		.	March	1942
Third (revised) edition		.	.	September	1943
Fourth edition	.		.	August	1945
Fifth (revised) edition		.	.	February	1949
Sixth edition	.	.	.	April	1955

Made and printed in Great Britain
by Wyman & Sons, Ltd., London, Fakenham and Reading.

CONTENTS

INTRODUCTION TO THE SERIES

It has been well said that 'the chief value of great men is to fertilise the imagination of adolescents'. Experience proves that biographical material is by far the most suitable for character-forming work among younger adolescents; hence the preparation of the brief biographical sketches issued in this series of 'Yarns' books.

The need is urgent to-day that the young adolescent should be helped to realise that life is not lived in water-tight compartments, and that every activity and legitimate interest in the complicated and many-sided life of our time should be impregnated with the Christian spirit. There is also the danger that the glamour of missionary adventure amid foreign scenes, and at that distance which is said to lend enchantment to the view, may make Christian work at home seem dull and uninviting in contrast. Therefore, while missionary Yarns have occasionally been included, the homeland is usually chosen as the sphere of service described. Both spheres of Christian service should of course be portrayed to eager youth.

The notes at the end of the book are intended to provide the Leader with certain information that is not conveyed in the Yarn itself. Suggestions for discussion after the Yarn has been told have been included, but these indicate a method rather than cover all the ground. The yarns should never be told without an opportunity for question and discussion being given.

E. H. H.

I

IGNATIUS

A CHRISTIAN LEADER WHO CHOSE MARTYRDOM

THE Roman Emperor and the Syrian bishop stood face to face. Each eyed the other with curiosity, for each represented a mighty force in the world, and both knew that this was the hour of crisis.

'What do you seek of me?' demanded the Emperor Trajan, looking down from his magnificent height at the shorter and slighter-built figure of the bishop. There was scorn in his tones, for he despised these Christians who professed a new religion, yet were too cowardly to fight for it.

'I come to warn you against trusting in the gods of Rome, who are no gods at all,' replied Ignatius boldly. 'It is folly to look to the gods of Rome for victory. It is worse than folly to harry and persecute the faithful followers of the one true God and His only Son, Jesus Christ.'

At these quiet words, spoken boldly as though between equals, the Roman Emperor turned livid with rage. Unused to anything but flattery and cringing obedience, the Emperor poured upon the bishop an angry torrent of abuse and threats. To his amazement, Ignatius stood his ground, uncowed.

'That is not how you should address one who carries Christ in his heart,' said Ignatius quietly.

'Do you mean that Jewish felon who was crucified by Pilate?' sneered the Emperor.

'Yes,' said Ignatius, 'for it is written, "I will live in

5

them and walk in them." For many years have I served Him, and He dwells within me.'

Without another word, the Emperor turned on his heel and addressed a sharp order to the Roman guard who stood at attention behind them.

'Take this man and keep him fast.'

As the bishop was marched from the Emperor's presence, Trajan dictated his decree of punishment to a scribe: 'We give orders that Ignatius, who asserts that he carries about within himself the Crucified One, be put in bonds under the custody of soldiers and carried to great Rome to be food for the wild beasts and to make sport for the people.'

Later that same day the Emperor's decree was read to the bishop in his dungeon below. To the amazement of his guards, Ignatius exclaimed: 'I thank Thee, O Master, that Thou has deigned to honour me with perfect love towards Thee, binding me thus with iron bonds in fellowship with Thy Apostle Paul.'

The news of the arrest and condemnation of the Bishop of Antioch spread like wildfire. It smote dismay into the hearts of the Christians in the ancient city, who were now left leaderless in a time of crisis. Among the imperial soldiers, however, gathered in great numbers in the city, the news spread great joy. Here was another token that would bring the favour of the gods to Trajan's new enterprise.

Trajan himself followed up this victory over the Christians by instant action. Orders were issued that all who would not attend the public worship of the gods should be tortured and put to death. The 'impudent folly' of the leader of the Christians, in thus seeking out the Emperor, had saved his soldiers the trouble of hunting him out and arresting him.

The Emperor now turned his attention to completing

his plan of campaign against the Parthians. The gods had given him a great victory over his enemies on the Danube; nothing should now be left undone to secure their favour for another triumph on the Euphrates. So part of his preparations for victory was a great campaign to appease the gods by stamping out the new religion, since the undutiful behaviour of the Christians might well cause offence to the very gods whose favour he sought.

A few days later, a terrible earthquake smote Antioch, the second capital of the Empire, causing great consternation among the people and much loss of life. The Christians, hiding in the city, regarded the earthquake as a sign of the Divine vengeance against the Roman persecutor, and hoped it might turn him from his purpose. On the contrary, however, Trajan was more wrathful than ever against the despised followers of the Nazarene, whose existence was an affront to the gods. 'Away with the Christians' was the order again issued, and the hunting out of men, women and little children, and the butchery of the followers of Christ, went on with greater zest than ever. Yet, fired to loyalty by the bold example of their beloved bishop, the Christians stood fast by their new faith.

A few days later, the proud Emperor rode out of Antioch at the head of his army to destroy the Parthians. Soon afterwards, Ignatius, in chains and surrounded by an armed guard, was marched to the quay to begin the long journey to Rome, with a cruel death awaiting him at the end. Yet, strange to relate, the victorious Emperor faced east troubled in spirit, while the condemned prisoner faced west with the light of victory in his face and a great joy in his heart.

Looking back, Ignatius felt that he had been prepared for this hour. Called in young manhood from a life of sin and selfishness, and won to Jesus Christ by the Apostle John himself, his gifts of leadership had soon made him prominent in the Church in Antioch, where Paul himself had laboured not many years before.

So tireless had he been in proclaiming the Good News of Christ in that cosmopolitan and evil city, that when Bishop Evodius had passed to his reward, Ignatius had been chosen by general consent as his successor. Ignatius had thrown himself into the work of extending the cause of Christ in Antioch, since it was a centre of Roman life and government second only to the Imperial City itself. So successful had he been that many had turned from the worship of the gods to serve Christ. No wonder that the priests in the heathen temples of the city, and the makers of idols, had learned to hate his very name.

How thankful was the bishop now that in the hour of crisis so many of the Christians had remained faithful, despite Trajan's fierce persecution. Thus in the very hour when the Emperor needed to appease the gods most, many stout-hearted Christians had refused to worship the gods, or to offer incense before the statue of the Emperor. Their very disobedience had sent the Emperor forth with troubled face on his new expedition, even while it had rejoiced the heart of the chained bishop, so that a horrible death in the arena at Rome had no terrors for him.

Few men have been called upon to face such an ordeal as Ignatius on that journey by sea and land to Rome. Week after week he had to endure the indignation and suffering of enforced travel in chains, surrounded by a hostile guard. 'It was like fighting with wild beasts all the way to Rome,' he told some of his friends at a later stage of the journey.

Yet for six long weeks he endured it, well knowing that a word from him of disloyalty to Christ would have brought him freedom. He need only have 'showed willing' to worship the gods to save his life and secure his freedom. Yet not for one minute did he harbour the thought of disloyalty to his Master.

There are many points of resemblance between his journey to Rome and that of the revered Apostle Paul not many years earlier. Like Paul, Ignatius was allowed to have the company of two friends—Philo and Aga-thopus. The first stage of the journey was by ship, but at Smyrna a halt had to be made. It was late in the season and no ship was ready to sail to the coast of Italy. The centurion in charge of the party chafed at the delay, but to Ignatius it was ordered of the Lord, since it gave him a period of happy fellowship with his old friend, Polycarp, the Bishop of Smyrna.

The stay of Ignatius in Smyrna was like a halt in a triumphal procession. Not only did Polycarp visit him, seeking guidance and strength in the Lord, but the Christians of Smyrna, stirred by the tragic situation of the famous Bishop of Antioch, visited him and showered kindnesses upon him. Delegations from the churches in provincial towns, hearing of Ignatius's enforced stay in Smyrna, also came to see him. In those days of waiting, the prison-chamber of Ignatius in Smyrna must have been like Paul's hired house in Rome—a centre of Christian fellowship and joy.

Through the visitors who came to see him, Ignatius sent many messages of cheer and strength to the Christians of Asia Minor. At this period he also wrote more than one epistle to the Churches, and these reveal the high-hearted gallantry of this pioneer-martyr.

'Leave me to become the prey of the beasts, that by their means I may be accounted worthy of God,' he wrote. 'I am the wheat of God, and by the teeth of the beasts I shall be ground, and I hope that I may be found

A*

to be the pure bread of God. Pray for strength to be given to me from within and from without, that I may not only speak, but also be willing, and that I may not merely be called a Christian, but may also be found to be one.'

Thus the visit of the bishop in chains to Smyrna proved to be a great strengthening and heartening to the entire Christian brotherhood in that part of the empire. Fired by the iron faith and glowing loyalty of Ignatius, many a waverer was confirmed in the new way of life and stood firm under persecution in his witness for Christ.

Possibly the great triumph of Ignatius's enforced stay in Smyrna caused the Roman centurion to cut short their visit, for when no boat appeared to take them by sea, the officer with his prisoner hurried overland to Troas, hoping to find a ship there to take them across the Ægean.

Here again, however, the party was doomed to delay. No boat was sailing to Europe, and although this prolongation of the journey to death must have had its trying side to Ignatius, it was regarded by him as due to the good ordering of the Lord. It gave the prisoner time to write a brotherly epistle to Polycarp, and to hear the good news that his own people at Antioch had been relieved from further persecution. In an epistle written at the time, he rejoices that to his own breast are to be gathered the spears of Roman persecution, and that through his sufferings his beloved flock in Antioch would escape the scourge.

At last the famous city on its seven hills came in sight and the last bit of road was traversed. On reaching Rome, Ignatius was met by the leaders of the Church there, who welcomed him with mixed feelings. They had recently lost their beloved bishop, Clement, who had been a disciple of the apostles themselves. It was with rare joy, therefore, that they welcomed to their city one who had been a disciple of the Apostle John. But the prospect that death would soon snatch him from their midst sobered their exhilaration.

Some of them, indeed, begged his permission to intercede with the authorities on his behalf. Surely he had suffered so much through this long and trying journey for his faith, that the sentence of death might be revoked, or at least suspended pending an appeal to the Emperor!

But to such suggestions Ignatius turned a deaf ear. Not for one moment would he allow them to impede the course of events, or beg for the slightest delay in the execution of the Emperor's sentence. He was eager to seal his faith with his blood, hoping thereby not merely to demonstrate his own loyalty to Christ, but to strengthen the faith of others by his last witness.

When at last the aged bishop was hurried off to the Colosseum, the games were nearly over. The vast amphitheatre, however, was still filled with a dense crowd representing all classes. Magistrates, city fathers, senators, nobles, and fine ladies, as well as a great concourse of citizens, sat tier upon tier enjoying the sight of beasts fighting to the death and gladiators being butchered to make a Roman holiday. A great shout of joy went up from the multitude when it was announced that the Christian bishop from Antioch would be brought in.

'Ignatius for the lions! The Christian bishop for the lions!' yelled the delighted mob. Amid the gloating of the populace, the old man was led out to face the wild beasts. It is said that, as they rushed upon him, he prayed for his enemies: 'Lord, lay not this sin to their charge; they know not what they do.'

Glorying in the fact that he was dying for the Name of Christ, Ignatius welcomed the beasts with a smile. In a few minutes, all was over, the two deacons who had followed their beloved bishop from Antioch to the amphitheatre in Rome reverently gathered up his bones after the games were over, and bore them back to his own city for burial.

Ignatius himself would make no claim to distinction as a martyr for Christ, for thousands of Christians, during the stormy days when Rome was trying to stamp out the Christian faith, paid for their loyalty with their lives. Yet no martyr left a deeper impression on the Early Church than did Ignatius, who travelled gladly for six weeks to face death for the sake of the Name.

Questions for Discussion.

Why was Ignatius made Bishop of Antioch?

Why did he seek audience of the Emperor Trajan?

How did he strengthen the Christians of Antioch in a time of persecution?

Was his journey to Rome a severer test for his faith and courage than facing death in the arena?

What bearing has Rev. 2. 8–10 on the story of Ignatius?

For Leaders' Notes on this yarn, see page 84.

II

TELEMACHUS

WHO GAVE HIS LIFE TO END GLADIATORIAL FIGHTS

Telemachus, the hermit, knelt on sharp-pointed stones in prayer. The sun blazed in well-nigh intolerable heat upon the bare mountain-side; the mouth of the cave that was his hermitage showed dark against the glitter of the rocks, but by day he never entered its shade. His single, coarse garment was torn and frayed; his hair, matted and ill-kempt, hung over a face that was lined with pain.

Even now his knees were bleeding, but he hardly noticed it. His eyes—deep, burning eyes—were fixed on the rude cross, at the foot of which he was kneeling.

'My Lord! My Lord!' he cried. Tense and only half-conscious from the strain of his ecstasies of intercession, he could find no other words. What more could he bring, what more offer to his Lord?

In the sunset light, the tall cross shone red as if with spilt blood. Telemachus, dragging himself to his feet, gazed at it in awe. The self-wrought emotions of his fierce praying died away; very still, as if waiting, listening, he stood before the sign of a Life that had been given utterly for men. The stillness that had settled upon Telemachus gathered itself into a question for which there were no words. It was the question of his whole life; and this time he found the answer:

> 'Wake,
> Thou deedless dreamer, lazying out a life
> Of self-suppression, not of self-less love!'

Had it been that? In that moment of revelation,

Telemachus never questioned it. Into those years of self-torture, of self-imposed isolation, of fierce discipline and fiercer prayer, he had poured all his energies, but he had abided to himself alone. He had tried to suppress himself, to find God Himself, God—those had been the two words that had filled his life. But 'self-less love!' Why, he had deliberately left behind those others whose needs might have claimed his time and his interest, his endeavours and his service—in short, his love. The cities, full of men and women, were places of sin, but oh, he saw now that they were places of need!

The cross rose dark against the emerald light of the afterglow. Having lived for men among men, Jesus had died among men for men. Telemachus turned to look back down the rough track that led valley-wards. And in his heart he cried: 'The call of God.'

When the eagle wheeled out over the precipice in the light of the next dawning, there was no stir outside the hermit's cave, for Telemachus had started back to the world he had left.

> 'He set his face
> By waste and field and town of alien tongue
> Following a hundred sunsets and the sphere
> Of westward wheeling stars.'

For the cry that had sounded in his heart seemed ever clearer; and he knew that he must go to the city of all cities, where men's sin and men's need were greatest, to Rome itself. The journey was long and hard, but Telemachus cared nothing for hardships. He begged his food, he slept under the stars, here and there he found those who spoke to him reverently as to a holy man, for he still wore his hermit's robe; others cursed him and mocked. But he went on, on, on.

At last, seas crossed and more miles tramped than may be reckoned, he came to Rome itself. Its streets

were full of excited crowds; they hardly turned to gaze
at the strange figure of Telemachus, for holy men and
pilgrims were common in Rome. Anxious days had
been passed in Rome, until the glad news came that
the Roman general Stilicho had met and defeated the
Goths in a hard battle in the north of Italy, and had
driven them back to the mountains. The Roman populace was wild with delight, and the Senate voted that
the victor should be accorded a 'triumph,' after the
manner of the old days. But instead of visiting the
heathen temples as formerly, the churches were now
visited and thanks returned for the victory. Now, too,
there was no slaughter of the prisoners of war as in the
old days. A Christian State could not kill men in cold
blood. To finish the celebrations the usual games were
arranged in the Colosseum.

Because he was a holy man no question was asked
of him as he went in with the crowd and climbed to a
seat in that vast building, where the greatest attraction
of that day was to be the gladiatorial contests. The
Christian State that would not kill its prisoners, allowed
its own citizens and their slaves to kill each other to make
a show for thanksgiving and pleasure. Was that Christian? No one had ever raised the question whether Christ
would ask for such things to be done where He reigned.

'Among men, for men'—the words were ever in the
hermit's heart as he surveyed these heedless, bustling,
self-absorbed people. As he looked at this face or that,
he thought to himself: 'This is a man for whom Christ
died; that is one whom my Master loves.' There welled
up in his heart a great pity for their forgetfulness, a great
love for them, a great longing to serve them.

He found himself one of eighty thousand, seated tier
upon tier round the vast oval of the arena where, a
hundred years before, the Christians had been thrown to

the lions while Rome looked on and laughed. But Rome had been Christian now for eighty years; the Emperor was Christian and the bishop was second only to him. Far below, on that oval of yellow sand, five chariots were racing; Telemachus noticed them less than he noticed the crowd in whose various life he felt so deep a share. There was a stir about him; all leaned forward; a new eagerness lit the faces that peered down, and the light was not beautiful, but dark.

A band of men had marched into the arena; before the imperial stand they stopped; their shout came thinly up to him because of the distance: 'Hail, Caesar: we who are about to die, salute thee!'

The crowd leaned forward in growing intentness; soon there would be human wounds to watch, and a death-blow to cheer, as one gladiator killed another for the pleasure of the crowd.

> 'He beheld
> The dust send up a stream of human blood,
> And gladiators moving toward their fight,
> And eighty thousand Christian faces watch
> Man murder man.'

Rome was Christian now, but in Rome men, whom God loved, killed others whom God loved as dearly, all to make pleasure for eighty thousand more, whose birth-right was to be sons of God, too.

Telemachus knew now why he had been called to the city of cities. Did the cross shine there in the blood-stained arena before him, as he sprang over the parapet and dropped on to the trampled sand? His feet recog-nised the feel of it; he stumbled, was up, and the vast audience checked its cheer. In that moment of silence, his voice carried to the farthest tier:

> 'Forbear;
> In the great Name of Him Who died for men,
> Christ Jesus!'

He was among the gladiators, his face bright with the love he was proclaiming; one or two sword-arms fell to men's sides. An impatient murmur rose from the crowd: 'Let the games go on.' Still Telemachus stood between the gladiators, frail and yet possessed by a mighty power that for one moment held the eighty thousand still.

The gladiators thrust the old man aside, and went on with their contest, but Telemachus again forced his way between them. Now the crowd began to throw stones at the old man, and shouted angrily to the gladiators to kill him. The prefect in charge of the games gave the necessary command to the gladiators, and the next moment the old hermit was struck down by the sword. Telemachus had been martyred for Christ.

Why? To show that human life is sacred in the sight of God. At the sight of the hermit's dead body the crowd were silent, for he was a holy man, and they had been responsible for his death. They were shocked into thought. They realised now that their sport had been at the expense of other men's lives. The savagery of their pastimes had been shown them, and the contests came to an abrupt end.

To remind Christian Rome that every man is of infinite value to God, that each is the brother beloved of all, Telemachus had given his life. 'Greater love hath no man than this, that a man lay down his life for his friends.' His dream became a deed that woke the conscience of the world.

Questions for Discussion.

What made Rome (nominally Christian), tolerate human bloodshed and death in the name of amusement?

Why did the death of Telemachus end these gladiatorial scenes?

How can we show to-day that human life is sacred?

In what way can exploitation, bad housing, competitive business, or war debase the value of human life?

What bearing has Matthew 5. 21–24, 16. 25–26, on this story of Telemachus?

III

AUGUSTINE OF HIPPO

WHO DISCOVERED THE SOURCE OF TRUE HAPPINESS

AMONG the schoolboys of Tagaste, a small town in North Africa, during the last days of the Roman Empire, was a lad named Augustine, who liked his lessons, but had a horror of being punished. His mother had tried her hardest to persuade him to be a Christian, but he would have none of it.

In those days to be a Christian meant giving up all fun and pleasure, and most of the joys of ordinary life, so Augustine determined to enjoy himself instead. Yet, because his mother believed in prayer, he used to pray to God that he might not be flogged by his schoolmaster. These prayers did not avail, because his love of pleasure and adventure often led him into mischief. His father wanted him to be a teacher, and spent more than he could afford on the boy's education, but Augustine shirked many of his lessons in the pursuit of pleasure.

One day he stole some apples, not because he wanted them, but out of pure love of mischief. The apples were green and poor, and he threw them away, because he had plenty of better apples of his own.

'What I wanted to enjoy was not the thing I stole, but the actual sin of theft,' he confessed afterwards. He never forgot that escapade, because the joy of stealing proved a great disappointment.

Soon after this, Augustine's father scraped together enough money to send him to the city of Carthage, because he would have better chances there for his studies.

Carthage, however, proved to be an open door, not only to learning, but to new and dazzling pleasures.

The result was that Augustine not only gave himself up to the pleasures of the gladiatorial shows, but was drawn into evil ways by the bad companions he met there, for in the theatre of those days 'evil bubbled up like a frying-pan.' The sins he committed at this period stained his life afterwards, yet all the time he was conscious of a sense of shame. Even in his worst acts of evil the memory of his saintly mother haunted him, and he found no satisfaction or real pleasure in evil-doing.

Sometimes he did work hard, for he was ambitious and wanted to make a name for himself as a teacher. And it was through his study of books by older and steadier thinkers that he began to realise that there might be more in life than having a good time.

At the age of twenty-one, Augustine returned to his home-town to teach, and was sincerely trying to find answers to such deep questions as 'What am I?' 'Why am I in the world?'

Nothing that pleasure offered him really gave satisfaction. His mother still pleaded with him to become a follower of Jesus Christ, but he could not bear to give up his pleasures, unworthy and evil as he knew them to be. In this unsettled state of mind, he left home to take up work as a professor at Milan, in Italy. There he made a new friend in Ambrose, the famous and saintly bishop of that town, who looked after the brilliant newcomer, and treated him as a personal friend. As a result, Augustine went to hear Ambrose preach.

'At first,' he tells us, 'I thought how eloquently he speaks'; gradually there entered this other thought— 'how truly he speaks.' Stage by stage the difficulties which had hedged Augustine in seemed to be clearing away; his mother came from Africa to live with him in

Milan, and she helped him a great deal. He made other Christian friends in Milan, and they helped him. All that was wanting was the last step that would take him heart and soul into the company of the servants of Jesus Christ.

For long Augustine could not take that step, though as he listened to this great Christian bishop who had given up everything to follow Christ, he was smitten with shame at his own weakness. One morning in his garden, things came to a head.

'How long? How long?" his heart seemed to be crying out. 'To-morrow and to-morrow; why not *now*, why not let this hour be an end to my uncleanness?'

Just then he heard the voice of a child next door, reading aloud a lesson perhaps; the words he caught were: 'Take up and read, take up and read.'

The simple words seemed like a message, and when he took up his New Testament to obey and read, his eyes fell on these words: 'Not in rioting and drunkenness, not in debauchery and evil, not in strife and envying; but put ye on the Lord Jesus Christ.'

All his doubts and fears and misgivings fell away from him; at last Augustine took God at His word, and became Christ's man from that moment.

The news that Augustine had become a Christian spread among his friends like wildfire. His mother fell on her knees in thanksgiving to God, because the prayers of thirty-one years had been answered at last. When Easter came, he was baptized by Ambrose, rejoicing that he had found peace in his heart, truth in his mind, and joy in his life, by giving up selfish pleasure and indulgence, and devoting his life to the service of Jesus Christ. Then he went back to Africa, and spent four years in quiet service for Christ, for he had renounced the ambitions of the world, and was content to live very humbly.

But Augustine had brilliant gifts, and although he

knew it not, they were to be used in the service of the Church. One day he went on a visit to Hippo, an important town in North Africa, and went to the church there to worship. As he entered, he found the bishop, Valerius, in the act of telling his people that another presbyter (or teacher) must be chosen. Recognising Augustine, the people chose him there and then, and he was ordained presbyter of Hippo. So successful was he in this work that fearing lest some other church might secure him, Bishop Valerius appointed him assistant-bishop. When Valerius died some years afterwards, Augustine was appointed bishop, a post that he occupied with great success and usefulness until his death.

In the service of Christ, Augustine found ample scope for his gifts as a teacher, and great joy in helping others in Christ's Name. He built a hospice for strangers, was tireless in his care of the poor, and sold some of the church plate in order to ransom some captives. Above all, he took up his pen to teach by his books people whom he could not reach by his voice—books that have been of enormous help to the followers of Christ through all the centuries since.

So lived Augustine, Bishop of Hippo, having given himself freely and completely at last to the following of Jesus Christ. In the days when he had followed his own whims, seeking only his own pleasure, his life had been torn with doubts, and he had been restless, unhappy, unsatisfied. Looking back afterwards, he tells us that he could understand why that was—'Thou madest us for Thyself, O God, and our hearts are restless until they find their rest in Thee.'

Questions for Discussion.

Why did Augustine find no real satisfaction in pleasure and self-indulgence?

Why was he attracted to Bishop Ambrose?

How did he finally find the truth, and peace for his soul?

How did Augustine use his gifts in service for Christ?

How can we enjoy life and be followers of Jesus?

How does the story of Augustine illustrate Galatians 5. 16–23?

IV

ANSKAR

THE APOSTLE TO THE BARBARIC NORTHLANDS

In the rough old days in Europe, eleven hundred years ago, a boy named Anskar was born under the shadow of the famous French monastery at Corbei, near Amiens. The blood of the French nobility flowed in his veins. When only five years old his mother died, and this made a very deep impression on his mind.

A remarkable dream decided his calling. In his sleep he fancied himself struggling along on miry and slippery ground, beyond which lay a beautiful meadow. Then he beheld a lady of stately form, in rich attire, surrounded by others in white apparel, among them his mother. He strove to reach her, but the mire clung round his feet, and he could not struggle onward. The soft voice of the majestic lady thus addressed him:

'My son, wouldst thou join thy mother?'

'Most certainly do I wish it,' replied the boy.

'He who would come to us must flee those vanities which we abhor,' was the reply.

From that moment young Anskar, forsaking all sport and gaiety, devoted his time to prayer and study. In those days, the only way in which a youth could give himself to the work of religion was by entering a monastery and training to become a monk. Quite naturally, Anskar entered the famous monastery of his birthplace, later going to Mayence in Germany. He became a most industrious and successful scholar.

When he reached manhood, Anskar felt called to

devote his life to the spread of the Gospel amongst the heathen. Jesus Christ appeared to him in a vision, and called him to confess his sins that he might receive forgiveness. He replied: 'Thou knowest all things, not a thought is hidden from Thee.'

Then the Lord said: 'It is true that I know all things, yet it is My will that men should confess to Me their sins, that they may be forgiven.' When Anskar confessed, Christ pronounced his sins forgiven, in words that filled him with inexpressible joy. Then, like Paul of old, Anskar said: 'Lord, what wouldst Thou have me to do?' to which came the reply: 'Go, preach the word of God to the tribes of the heathen.'

It so happened that at that time Harold, king of Jutland, visited Germany, and while there was converted to Christianity, and baptized at Mayence. He soon felt that as Christianity helped him so much, and made his life so happy, all his subjects must share in his great discovery, so he asked for a volunteer to go back with him to take the new faith to his people. At first no one could be found to respond, for it meant going to a strange country, living among savage people, and travelling hundreds of miles by land, and crossing the sea, where the fierce pirates of the North might have to be faced.

At last, however, Abbot Wala, head of the monastery at Mayence, said he knew the very man, a young monk named Anskar. So the king sent for Anskar and put the challenge before him. It was no light task with which Anskar was faced, and which all others had refused. He knew that at that time practically the whole of Scandinavia, Finland and Iceland were occupied by the Northmen.

These fierce people were a Germanic race, some of whom lived by agriculture, but many more made their living by piracy. These pirates, or vikings, used to hover about in the bays on the coast, in order to pounce upon any ships that came along and plunder them. They had made themselves so feared that people dared not even approach their countries.

But Anskar was undismayed by the prospect, for he had been called by Jesus Christ to go and preach to the heathen. In reply to King Harold, he declared that he was not afraid of the pirates, or any other dangers, and would go back with him to Jutland and help to spread Christianity among his subjects. As soon as his friends heard that Anskar had agreed to go, they tried to discourage him, but he replied that he had received a definite call from God, and so refused to think of the dangers. His courage soon bore fruit, for at the last moment his friend Autbert, steward of the monastery, offered to go with him, and to help him with his work.

The great day came when Anskar, with much joy in his heart, set out with Autbert for the heathen land in the north. Travelling overland to Cologne, he was presented with a small ship by Bishop Hadebold, and in this he sailed down the Rhine and round the Netherlands to Jutland. Fortunately, he seems to have missed the pirates on this journey, and eventually landed at Schleswig. Here he set to work at once and, collecting some boys round him, started to teach them about Jesus Christ. He soon had a school of twelve children—the first in Jutland.

Unfortunately, the king was over-zealous, and tried to force Christianity on his subjects by destroying their temples. Naturally this did more harm than good, and only retarded Anskar's progress, but with his friend Autbert he worked on quietly for two years. Then came a great setback. His friend was taken ill and had to return to France, where he died.

Anskar was now left alone in a heathen country among

fierce people who were getting more and more angry because the king was trying to force them to give up their gods. The trouble grew rapidly worse, until the people rose in a body against the king and drove the Christians out of the country. Anskar, much against his will, was forced to flee to France. In accordance with his Master's orders, when persecuted in one country he fled to another. This time to Sweden.

Anskar had often longed to go to Sweden and to preach there. About this time the way was suddenly opened. In 829, messengers came to the king of France saying that they would like a missionary sent to Sweden. At first the king was nonplussed, but suddenly he remembered Anskar, and asked him if he would go. Needless to say, Anskar jumped at the chance, even though Sweden was an entirely unknown land and the prospect was full of peril. He set out with another monk named Witmar. To reach their destination they had to cross the Sound, where pirates abounded

This time, Anskar was not to escape scot-free. As they were nearing the Swedish coast, a band of pirates swept down on their ship. In the confusion of the moment when the pirates boarded the vessel, Anskar and his friend jumped overboard and swam for the shore, which they reached in safety. Through this misadventure the would-be ambassador for Christ was cast ashore like driftwood on the coast of Sweden. He and Witmar had lost all they possessed, especially their treasure of forty books (very rare in those days). They were, of course, without clothes or money.

What was to be done? Should they turn back? 'No,' said Anskar. So they continued their journey, and finally landed at Birka, near Stockholm. Here they were kindly received, and found that some Christian slaves had already prepared the way by telling others about Christ. After only eighteen months' work they converted Herigar, the chief of the king's counsellors, who built the first Christian church in Sweden on his estate.

When King Louis heard of Anskar's success, he made him Archbishop of Hamburg. But Anskar did not forget the people he had learned to love. He made his nephew Bishop of Sweden and sent him to carry on the work.

Anskar was not to be allowed to spend many years in peace as Archbishop of Hamburg. In those troublous days the Northmen were constantly invading and pillaging other lands. One day a band of these marauders surprised Hamburg and captured the city, Anskar barely escaping with his life, his collection of books being burnt to ashes. He took refuge in Bremen for a time, continuing his work as a bishop and elder of the Church.

In the meantime, an insurrection had broken out in Sweden against the king, who had been favourable to the Christians, and against the missionaries themselves. One Christian teacher suffered martyrdom, and the Bishop (Gauzbert) was seized and expelled from the country. For seven years paganism reigned unopposed. Then once again Anskar set sail for Sweden, in the hope of being able to persuade the king to allow him to recommence teaching the Christian religion.

He invited the king to a feast, and gave him many presents. But this time the king, more cautious and timid than before, declared that he must consult his people and his gods on so great a question. He called a private council of his nobles, who agreed to consult the gods by lot. The oracle was favourable to the acceptance of Christianity.

The whole of the people were then assembled in their parliament. A herald proclaimed the object of the meeting—the admission or rejection of Christianity by the nation. Opinions were conflicting, and tumult had almost begun when an aged man arose and declared that the God of the Christians had been singularly powerful in saving him and others from the peril of the sea, and from pirates.

'It would be much wiser, since our own gods are not always so favourable, to have this God also, who is so mighty and so ready a Protector,' he declared. This prudent advice carried with it the whole assembly, and Christianity was admitted by general consent. The start thus made enabled Anskar and other missionaries to gain ground slowly, but surely.

When he died, at the age of sixty-four, Anskar had succeeded in establishing Christianity throughout Sweden, and had also started the work again in Denmark. As a result of his labours the Gospel also spread into Norway about a century later. He is one of the almost-forgotten pioneers of the Gospel in Northern Europe. He had persevered in his task in face of all difficulties, dangers and opposition.

Questions for Discussion.

How was Anskar called to serve Jesus Christ?
Why was he ready to accompany King Harold to Jutland?
What did Anskar have to sacrifice when he went?
What were the dangers he faced?
Why did he think God meant him to go?
Where else did he labour for the Gospel?
What were the results of his work?
Suggest other examples of similar pioneer missionaries?
How does 2 Cor. 11. 23–31 summarise Anskar's labours?

V

JOHN HUSS

CHAMPION OF CHRISTIAN TRUTH AND LIBERTY

ONE winter evening, many years ago, a group of university students sat around the fire enjoying themselves in the city of Prague. One of their number, however, was deeply intent on the book he was reading. Presently he stretched forth his hand, put it into the fire, and held it there until one of his companions seized his arm to pull it away.

'Dost want to kill thyself, John of Husinetz?' he said.

For reply, John showed in his book the story of death by burning of Brother Lawrence, the martyr, and then said: 'I was only trying if I could bear anything, of what that holy man suffered for Christ's sake.'

Some of those students never forgot that strange act of John Huss, for it explained much that happened to him in after-years. John was a poor man's son, but from his earliest days had been fired by a great desire for learning. After his father's death, his mother took him from his native village to Prague, the great univeristy city of Bohemia, hoping to get him educated there. She carried a goose and a cake as a gift to the university authorities, but to the chagrin of mother and son, the goose escaped from the basket on the way, and only the cake could be offered as a gift.

Huss succeeded in getting into the university, maintaining himself by chanting and doing menial work for the church. So poor was he that he had to live mostly on porridge, and had no spoon to eat with.

'I used to make a spoon of a piece of bread till I had done eating my porridge, and then I ate the spoon,' he wrote afterwards. He called evil men 'the devil's spoons, by means of which he devoured others and then he devoured them also.' When he was twenty-five years old, Huss realized his heart's desire and became a priest, teaching at the university. He was very proud of his priestly gown, and loved to play chess. But never did he forget how he had burned his hand in the fire when he was a student, and he still starved in order to buy books and attend lectures to make himself a better servant of Jesus Christ.

A year later, Huss was appointed preacher to Bethlehem Chapel, founded in Prague some years earlier by a prominent citizen for the preaching of the Gospel in the language of the people. This was work after his own heart, for though a loyal servant at that time of the Pope of Rome, Huss disliked intensely conducting the services of the Church in Latin, an unknown tongue to the people. To prepare his sermons, Huss became a close student of the New Testament, with quick results. Looking round at the degraded lives of the people of Prague, he realised how much they needed the Gospel message. Soon his preaching against the vice and evil of the people, and his stern denunciation of their wicked practices, made his name ring throughout the city and the district. People of all classes flocked to hear him; even the queen and the nobles attended his services. Founding all he said upon the Scriptures, Huss denounced evil among all classes, and changed the hearts and lives of a great number of people.

After two years of preaching at Bethlehem Chapel, something happened to change the course of Huss's life. Two English preachers arrived in Bohemia from Oxford, bringing with them the teaching of John Wycliffe, the English reformer. The emissaries of the Pope soon had these English preachers arrested, and they were forbidden to teach. Nothing daunted, however, they proceeded to draw two pictures on the wall of the house in which they were staying.

On one wall they drew a picture of Jesus entering into Jerusalem, meek, riding upon an ass. On the opposite wall they displayed the royal magnificence of a papal procession, with the Pope, adorned with a triple crown, in costly robes covered with precious stones, riding proudly on a richly caparisoned horse, with trumpeters heralding his approach, and followed by a brilliant crowd of cardinals, bishops and other prelates.

These pictures were so well drawn that they could tell their own story, and soon the people of Prague flocked to see them. The pictures caused so much stir that the preachers had to withdraw from the city. Among those who went to study these pictures and their meaning, was Huss. As he compared the humble and simple entry of Jesus into Jerusalem with the splendour and wealth of the procession of the Pope, he realised how far the prelates and the clergy of his day had departed from the simple method of Jesus Christ and His disciples.

These pictures led Huss to study the writings of John Wycliffe, with remarkable effect. All Prague was soon stirred by the new message of their popular preacher, for Huss boldly denounced the evil lives of the clergy and the Pope, contrasting them with the Gospel story, which he gave to the people in their own tongue. At once the Archbishop and clergy were up in arms against him. A certain priest, hiding his head in a grey mantle and cowl, attended the services at Bethlehem Chapel in order to find a cause for accusing Huss of heresy. His presence made no difference whatever to the fearless preacher, who guessed his mission. In the midst of an explanation of the difference between the laws of God and the laws of the Pope, Huss called out to the monk from the pulpit: 'Write that down, cowled monk, and carry it to the bishop's palace.'

Attempts were made by bribes and threats to silence Huss, but he could not be moved. Fearlessly he went on preaching the Gospel to the people, and exposing the evil lives of all classes. So great was his influence that when a new rector was required for the university at Prague, Huss was elected to that office. This gave him greater power than ever in Bohemia, and as a result of his preaching many reforms were made.

No matter how popular Huss became with the people of Bohemia, he nevertheless made many bitter enemies among clergy, bishops and other powerful prelates. At that time a determined effort was being made to stamp out in England all results of Wycliffe's work, and in the course of this campaign all copies of Wycliffe's books in circulation on the Continent were ordered to be given up and burnt. Over 200 books, many of them beautifully written and elegantly bound, were publicly burned in the streets of Prague. But nothing could stop John Huss preaching many of the truths that Wycliffe had proclaimed, inasmuch as they were based on Scripture.

Soon after this, Huss found a new opportunity for preaching his Gospel of reformation. In 1412, Pope John ordered a crusade against the King of Naples, who was supporting his rival, Pope Gregory. To help this crusade, Pope John promised forgiveness of sins in advance (papal indulgences) to all who would take part in the war or provide money for it.

When the Pope's legate came to Prague to sell these indulgences, this evil traffic was hotly denounced by Huss. The Pope now took action against him, and since he refused to stop preaching or to go to Rome to give an account of himself (which would have meant certain death), he was excommunicated, and the whole of Prague put under an interdict. This meant that the churches were closed and all religious work stopped. To preserve peace, therefore, Huss retired from Prague to the castle of one of his friends, and spent the time in writing books and pamphlets, which were scattered over the land and helped the work of reformation and religious liberty.

When every attempt to shut the mouth and stop the work of Huss had failed, the Pope decided to use other means. At that time a great Council of the Church was called at Constance, in Switzerland, to settle the claims of the rival Popes. It was determined to get Huss condemned by this Council. Accordingly, the King of Italy, the chairman of the Council, summoned Huss to attend, sending him a pledge of safe conduct to and from Constance. King Wenceslaus, his own sovereign, also pledged Huss a safe conduct. Huss went to Constance, but trusting not in kings.

'I confide altogether in the all-powerful God, my Saviour,' he declared. 'He will fortify me in His trust, that I may face with courage temptation, prison and, if necessary, a cruel death.' It is clear, therefore, that Huss knew how little faith could be put in the pledges of kings and princes.

Yet, knowing all the risks, he went boldly to Constance to face his accusers and deliver his message. Wherever he went he met with a friendly reception, but as soon as he arrived at Constance his enemies got to work. He was arrested and thrown into a filthy cell above a sewer. Here he was confined week after week, until he became so ill that his enemies, fearing he would die and so escape their vengeance, removed him to a better prison.

Several times Huss was brought before the Council,

but the tumult of his enemies was so great that he could not say a single word. After nine months' imprisonment he was brought before the Council and convicted of heresy. He was then taken to the cathedral in his robes of office and led, communion cup in hand, to the high altar. There the cup was taken away from him, his robes stripped from him, and he was led to the neighbouring meadows and burnt at the stake.

Even at the last moment he was urged to recant and save his life, but he replied boldly that he was willing to sign his testimony with his blood. As the flames rose around him, he was heard praying for the forgiveness of his enemies, and he died singing hymns.

His ashes were thrown into the Rhine so that no trace of his body remained. But nothing could stop the work of Huss. After his death, powerful friends carried on his work and his followers, called Hussites, followed up his teaching and kept the reformer's work going till the time of Luther and Tyndale.*

Questions for Discussion.

Why did Huss preach in the vulgar tongue?
What difference did his preaching make to the people of Prague?
Why did Huss pass on the teaching of Wycliffe?
Why was he burnt at the stake?
How did his work help forward the Protestant Reformation?
What do we learn from his life?
What bearing has Luke 9. 23-36 on this story?

* See Yarns on Wycliffe and Tyndale in *Yarns on Social Pioneers*, and on Luther in *More Yarns on Social Pioneers*, which should be read in connection with this Yarn.

B

VI

HUGH LATIMER*

POPULAR PREACHER OF THE REFORMATION

THE Wars of the Roses were nearing their last fight when a son was born to a Leicestershire yeoman, and given the name of Hugh Latimer. Hugh proved to be a delicate boy, but very quick at learning, so that he was encouraged to become a scholar rather than follow his father's footsteps on the land. The boy lived in stirring times, and remembered long afterwards the day when he helped to buckle the harness on his father's horse, as the yeoman went off to serve the king on Blackheath Field, where the brief rebellion of Perkin Warbeck was brought to an end.

Latimer's farm was a small one, rented at three or four pounds a year, and only able to employ half a dozen men. He had a walk for a hundred sheep and his wife milked thirty kine. Yet he was able to send his only son to school and to marry his daughters with a dowry of twenty nobles apiece.

Young Hugh promised so well at his studies that he was marked out for the Church, and by dint of much sacrifice his father sent him to the University of Cambridge. Those were great days for Cambridge, for in the early years of the fifteenth century it was thronged with young men eager to get 'the new learning,' as it was called. One of Latimer's college friends, Walter Bilney by name, introduced him to the new version of the Greek New Testament, which Master Erasmus, the hero of

* Based in part on notes by LILIAN E. COX, B.A.

every young scholar of the day, had just published. How clear it made many a difficult passage! Reading there, for the first time, many of those texts which we have come to take for granted (so well do we know them) Latimer found that many of the opinions he had taken without a thought must be given up. Bilney's favourite text was 1 Timothy i. 15: 'This is a faithful saying and worthy of all acceptation, that Christ Jesus came into the world to save sinners, of whom I am the chief!'

Yet the Church said that a priest's absolution was necessary to save sinners; the Church said that a man must pay money and buy an indulgence from the Pope if he would save himself from torture after death. If the coming to earth of Christ Jesus was the secret of salvation, how could these things be? Surely the Church had watered down that great Good News, thought Latimer.

Latimer was soon resolved to stand for the whole grand message of the Bible, and for nothing less. All round him he saw so-called priests who barely knew how to read, and were almost ignorant of the message they should proclaim. He saw other priests who were given up to luxury; many of them lived evil lives. He saw the ignorance and superstition of the ordinary people, and the selfishness and oppression of the rich; so this yeoman's son turned priest and flung himself into the battle for a new state of affairs.

Those in authority soon began to hear of his unconventional views; one day when he was preaching he saw no less a personage than the Bishop of Ely enter the church and sit to listen. Latimer guessed that the bishop had come to hear if anything unorthodox was being said, so he at once changed the topic of his sermon —but *not* to one likely to be acceptable to the bishop. His new theme was Christ as the pattern of all priests and bishops—and he looked straight at the bishop meaningly as he preached. The result was that Latimer was forbidden to preach in the university, or in any parish church of the diocese. Did that silence him? No. He gained permission from a friendly abbot, and carried on his campaign from the pulpit of a monastery church.

Before long, he gained an interview with King Henry VIII—not to secure any boon or preferment for himself —but to plead the cause of a poor woman who had been wrongfully imprisoned in Cambridge.

This brought him to the king's notice, and he was asked to London to preach before Henry, and given a parish in Wiltshire. He soon became famous for his preaching against the errors of the Church. The Bishop of London charged him with heresy, for preaching a sermon denouncing image-worship and the adoration of the Virgin Mary. Latimer almost wished that the sea was between him and the bishop, for often that charge meant death, and he took care to have a good time with his parishioners that Christmas, in case he never came back. He was brought before the Church court, but as he could agree to the questions they asked him, he was set free.

By and by he came to the king's notice in a different connection; he was appointed a member of the commission that was to go into the legality of Henry's proposed divorce from Catherine of Aragon, and since Latimer was one of those whose vote favoured the king's point of view, we are not surprised to learn that soon after he was appointed chaplain to the new queen, Anne Boleyn.

A prosperous and comfortable life might now have been his. But comfort was no ideal of Latimer's; he had a mission to perform and a message to deliver.

Above all, he wanted to secure an open Bible for the people of England. From this time forward Latimer probably did more to establish the Protestant Reformation in England than any other man. He had a gift for making his teaching live in the minds and hearts of his listeners. He had all the gifts of the popular orator, and was criticised even by those in sympathy with his views for his racy and popular method of preaching.

One Christmas time he set everyone talking by his famous 'Sermons on the Cards.' It was then, as now, the custom at Christmas time to play cards, and seizing upon this, Latimer announced that he would deal out to the people 'Christ's cards,' so that they might be winners and not losers in the game of life. The first 'card' Latimer dealt contained Christ's law of forgiveness (from the Sermon on the Mount, Matthew 5. 21, 22). The second 'card' dealt with the injunction to be reconciled to those who had done an injury (Matthew 5. 23, 24). Both these cards, the preacher declared, were often misunderstood and badly played, with the result that the game was lost.

These sermons, with such homely illustrations, made a great hit at the time, and called for a reply from the orthodox party. A Dominican prior attempted to answer by proposing to teach people the game of 'Christian dice,' and how to cast *cinque* and *quatre* to the confusion of Latimer's opinions. The prior's assault was aimed at Latimer's policy of the free circulation of the Scriptures in the common tongue. Unfortunately, the prior's wit was not equal to the brilliance of Latimer's humour.

Defending his own use of metaphor, and ridiculing the danger urged by the prior that the common people would misunderstand the metaphors of Scripture, Latimer pointed out that the metaphors were not confined to the

Scriptures. 'The very painters do paint them on walls and in houses as, for example'—and here he looked straight at the prior—'when they paint a fox preaching out of a friar's cowl, none is so mad as to take this to be a fox that preacheth, but know well enough that it is to point out to us what hypocrisy and craft lie hid in these friars' cowls, willing us thereby to beware of them.'

Thus the ready wit and powerful preaching of Latimer helped everywhere the great work of freeing the Scriptures for the common people, and ridding England of priestcraft and all that it stood for.

Latimer is also famous for the letter he sent to King Henry, urging the free circulation of the Holy Scriptures in the English tongue. It has been said that 'no nobler letter exists in the whole wide compass of English literature.' The historian Froude describes it as 'prose of almost unexampled grandeur.' The king was not prepared at the time to take the step urged upon him by Latimer in this letter, but this act was valuable as propaganda for the popularising of the Scriptures, and the king made Latimer one of his royal chaplains soon afterwards.

By this time Henry VIII had decided that the Pope had no right to demand taxation from Englishmen just because he was the head of the Church, so Henry announced that, as far as England was concerned, he himself was head of the Church. He further determined to abolish many of the monasteries and abbeys where, he declared, monks had been living in idleness and sometimes in luxury, supplying the Pope with great revenues which England could ill spare.

Certainly there was truth in the charges brought against the monasteries; Latimer, as a leader in reform, knew that. But he was essentially fair, and he saw another side, too. He was in London where the law was passed, and heard the Parliament shout in their excitement 'Down with them!' as the charges against the monasteries were read. But Latimer lamented that there was more plunder than reformation, and he spoke boldly about this to the nobles and to the king himself.

'It is not well,' he said, 'to use as royal stables buildings which were raised and maintained for the helping of the poor.' He accused those who had stolen the riches of this abbey church or that, for their own private use, and he who knew that a bishop should be chosen for the qualities that fitted him to be a good shepherd of the people, unceasingly condemned the king for turning some of the dispossessed abbots into bishops, just to save the cost of pensions.

By and by he was made Bishop of Worcester. He at once sent round to every priest under his charge, and by his message we can see not only his reforming spirit at work, but also gain an idea of the need for reform. Remember, this message was sent to those who were already priests: 'Every one of you,' he said, 'should obtain if possible the whole Bible; or at least the New Testament, in Latin or in English; and that before Christmas.'

Latimer knew from his own experience what an awakening comes upon men's spirits as they read the Bible for themselves; he believed that more could be done by getting people to read the Bible than by any amount of law-making or imprisoning. He felt it was wrong to defend the faith by sword and by force. 'For God,' he said, 'will have it defended not by man or man's power, but by His Word only, by which He hath evermore defended it, and that by a way far above man's power or reason.'

All this time Latimer was practising what he preached. He was a very busy man, for he gave himself unsparingly

to the affairs of his bishopric; but nothing was allowed
to hinder him from the Bible study and quiet prayer
which he knew were the mainspring of a Christian life.
Every morning he rose soon after 2 a.m. to study; he
mentions this in a letter written about 1552, when he
was an old man.

The general slackness and ignorance had made the
worship in the churches largely meaningless or filled
with superstition.

Men knew so little of God that they came to think
of religion as a mere matter of magic. In St. Paul's
Cathedral, in London, great veneration was paid to a
certain small statue of a saint. There it stood in its
niche, to all appearance just placed there; yet 'not
four yoke of oxen harnessed together could move it,'
the people vowed. Latimer preached a sermon, homely,
humorous, frank, to show them their mistake. He
did more; striding down from the pulpit, he took down
the image from its place while the awestruck people
watched, and carried it to the door, where he flung it
into the rubbish of the gutter. 'Worship God,' he
cried, 'and know that such man-made images have no
might.'

In his own cathedral of Worcester, he found a statue
of the Mother of Christ hung round with precious jewels
brought by those who sought God's help; they believed
that thus they could win Divine favour. As he taught
them the simple, straight way that is open from any
man's needy heart to the heart of a loving, listening
God, Latimer stripped the jewels from the image and
sold them to help the poor; later he had the statue
removed, lest any should again fall into that error. But
it was not only to poor country folk that Latimer preached
in these emphatic ways; the fashionable folk of the capital
flocked to hear him. The merchants had to hear straight

talks on such subjects as the duty of restoring stolen goods, but in spite of this—or perhaps because they admired his daring—the crowds continued. In 1549 there is an entry in the churchwarden's accounts of St. Margaret's, Westminster: '1s. 6d. for mending of divers pews broken when Dr. Latimer did preach!'

More than once his campaign for Christian truth brought him into clash with the authorities, and twice he was arrested and imprisoned in the Tower. By and by he was released, but he would not take up his bishopric again; he felt that he would be freer without it for preaching and for practical works that would help folk on. We feel we have a real sidelight on the temperament of this most lovable of reformers when we hear that when, for the last time, he took off his official robe as a bishop and laid it aside for ever, he skipped for joy.

Time soon brought great changes, however. In the reign of Queen Mary the supporters of the Pope once more came into power in England. Latimer knew that his work would now be challenged. A warrant was soon issued for his arrest; but popular feeling was all on the side of the preacher who had made such a mark on the life of the people of his day, and those who served the warrant were careful to let Latimer have advance information, hoping that he would escape. He refused to avail himself of this, however, and greeted the pursuivant with a smile: 'You are a welcome messenger,' he said. He was flung into the common jail at Oxford, and for a year suffered very great hardships there.

When the time came for his trial (in March, 1554), he was a bent, wasted figure, 'with a kerchief and cap on his head, his spectacles hanging by a string at his breast, staff in hand.' With Cranmer and Ridley he was accused of refusing to say mass or accept the Papal doctrines with regard to it. Ill and old, Latimer faced his accusers. 'I have had neither pen nor ink nor any book wherewith to prepare my defence,' he said. 'No book—save only the New Testament, which same I have read over seven times without finding the mass therein, nor yet the marrow-bones and sinews thereof.' Was he thinking then of those words to which Master Bilney had first pointed to him so long ago—'This is a faithful saying, and worthy of all acceptation, that Christ Jesus came into the world to save sinners'?

All three reformers were quickly found guilty of heresy, and condemned to death. The stake was erected in the open space before Balliol College, and there, on an autumn morning, Latimer and Ridley were bound among the faggots. Latimer's last words have rung down through history; they speak of a campaign that was not ending, but just beginning: 'Be of good cheer, Master Ridley, and play the man. We shall this day light such a candle by God's grace in England as I trust shall never be put out.' Then 'he received the fire as if embracing it.'

'Thus much,' says Foxe, the faithful chronicler of these heroic incidents, 'concerning the end of this old and ever-blessed servant of God, Bishop Latimer, for whose laborious services, fruitful life, and constant death the whole realm has cause to give thanks to Almighty God.'

Questions for Discussion.

Why did the reading of the New Testament lead to a reformation in religion?

In what way did Latimer help the Protestant Reformation?

Why was he an advocate of giving the Bible to the English people?

What was the 'candle' lighted by Latimer and Ridley?

How has it given light to the people?

Why were the Reformers impressed by the teaching of St. Paul in 1 Tim. 1?

VII

VINCENT DE PAUL

HERO OF THE GALLEY-SLAVES OF FRANCE

In the 16th century, a Gascony peasant lad named Vincent spent his days minding his father's small flock of sheep in the fields. Like David of old, he had plenty of time while guarding his sheep to study Nature, and to read the love of God in the fields, the trees, and the blue sky.

Every night on the way to his home, Vincent's road lay past a pool, shaded by a grove of oak trees, close by the ruins of a little chapel. While the sheep were drinking from the pool, Vincent would slip into the chapel to pray to God, and then would lead his flock home. When the winter days stopped his work, and the sheep were kept on the little farm, Vincent went to a school over the hills in the nearest village.

One day he went to the village very joyfully, taking thirty pence with him—the result of many weeks' savings —to buy something he wanted badly; but on the way to the shop he met a poor, starving beggar. Without hesitation he gave the thirty pence to the man to buy food, and returned home quite happy.

When he grew older, Vincent, after much thought, vowed that he would use his life in God's service, and spend his days in teaching the people about Jesus Christ. So he said goodbye to his parents, left the little farm, and went to college in a distant town, to study to become a minister of the Gospel.

When he had finished his studies, Vincent was travelling

in a little ship down the Mediterranean when the vessel
was chased by pirates and captured. Vincent and
everyone on board were taken prisoner and landed at
a port on the north coast of Africa. Loaded with heavy
chains, he was led through the streets with the other
prisoners to the slave-market, and there offered for sale.
The other prisoners were in despair, but Vincent was
cheerful and willing, because he had learned to trust
his life to God.

Attracted by his bright and cheerful face, a chemist
bought Vincent, and took him home to stoke the furnaces
in which the chemist heated his metals. For several
years Vincent proved a faithful slave, because he was a
loyal servant of God. When the chemist had to sell his
slaves, Vincent was bought by a farmer, and set to work
in the fields. Again he worked hard and cheerfully,
practising the Golden Rule and doing his best to help
others.

Soon his mistress became interested in him, because
he was so different from the other slaves. One day in
the fields, she heard him singing praises to God, as he
had learned to do when a shepherd.

'Sing me the praises of your God,' she asked him,
and Vincent sang to her.

Every day after that, she came to listen to Vincent,
and he talked to her about God and his Master, Jesus
Christ. The farmer's wife then told her husband about
his Christian slave, and before long the farmer (who
had been a Christian years before, but had turned his
back on Jesus Christ) became a Christian once again,
and determined to set Vincent free. So with his master
and mistress Vincent sailed back to France and regained
his liberty. Then he settled down among the poor, to
teach them about Jesus.

In those days slavery was common in France, and

because he had been a slave Vincent felt special pity for these men and longed to help them, knowing what they suffered. At that time men were sometimes made slaves because of quite small offences, and were condemned to row the great ships that belonged to France.

Vincent visited these unfortunate slaves in the filthy prisons, cheering and helping them. When they were taken to the galleys, the slaves were given caps to wear to mark their offences; grey for deserters, green for smugglers, and red for thieves.

Each of the slave-galleys had about three hundred rowers, three or four to one big oar, often fastened to their seats with heavy iron chains. Officers stood over them at intervals with great whips, and lashed them if they did not work well. If they tried to escape, they were severely punished.

Vincent went on board the galleys to talk with the slaves. One day he said: 'I will try to help these poor people,' so went to the admiral of the galleys, and told him what he had seen in the prisons and in the ships.

'I cannot see what can be done about it,' the admiral said.

'I can,' replied Vincent, 'let me try.'

Permission was given and Vincent went from prison to prison, encouraging and befriending the prisoners. He collected money for them, and even had those who were ill removed to a house which he had fitted up as a sort of hospital, to give them better conditions until they were restored to health and could be sent to the ships.

The men came to love him, and listened eagerly when he told them of Jesus Christ. Thus their lives, even though they were prisoners, were thereafter made happier because they saw that they could have another Master than the cruel galley officers.

One day Vincent was by the harbour-side in Marseilles trying to cheer the prisoners near a large galley which was just going to sail. As he was talking to them, he noticed a young man waiting to be taken on board, sobbing piteously.

'Why are you so sad?' said Vincent.

'Because of my wife and little children,' said the man. 'Without anyone to work for them, they will now starve.'

As Vincent talked with him, he suddenly saw a new way of being a friend to the prisoners and of serving his Master, Jesus Christ. In a moment, he had thrown his cloak over the man's shoulders, and stood himself bare-shouldered, with the prisoner's red cap on his head. Then he sent the man quickly home. When the officers came to march the galley-slaves on board, Vincent went with them. He was dragged aboard the galley and chained to his seat. Then he bent to his oar, and the vessel started.

As time went on, the work became harder, and the whips lashed upon the slaves, but Vincent pulled at his oar with a song in his heart, because of the gladness that came from helping a brother. By and by, it was discovered that this prisoner was Vincent, the friend of the slaves, and he was set free. He went back to his work of befriending the galley-slaves of France.

Ever since his day, the prisons of Europe have been less dreadful places, and the poor folk of France have been less miserable, because Vincent lived his life of love.

Questions for Discussion.

How did Vincent prove that he was a follower of Jesus?

Why did he champion the cause of the galley-slaves?

What made him take the place of the distressed slave on the quay?

How does his life-story illustrate Matthew 7. 12?

VIII

FRITZ OBERLIN

PIONEER OF EVERYDAY RELIGION

ONE day in the streets of Strasbourg (on the borders of France and Germany), a boy saw a policeman ill-treating a poor, crippled beggar. This injustice so angered him that he pushed the policeman away and railed at him for being so cruel. The policeman was about to march the boy off to the police station, when the crowd interfered, and he therefore had to let them both go. A few days later, the boy, who was called Fritz Oberlin, saw the same policeman approaching in a narrow street. 'Shall I turn tail and run?' he said to himself. 'No, I tried to help a poor cripple; God will now help me.' He stalked boldly past the policeman who, admiring his courage, smiled and passed on.

From his boyhood days, young Fritz was a rebel against injustice, a helper of the oppressed and needy, and a courageous follower of Jesus Christ. He was a hard worker at school, and because his father was poor, became a pupil-teacher in order to pay his fees at Strasbourg University.

From his early days, he had loved soldiering, and when he had finished his university career, Fritz accepted a post as military chaplain. One cold morning, a visitor came to see him. The man looked at the poverty-stricken room, and said: 'This looks like Rock Valley.'

He then explained these strange words by saying that he was the minister of Rock Valley in the Vosges Mountains, not many miles away. The hardships of

47

life in that bare and bleak valley had undermined his wife's health, and he was compelled to leave. He was now looking for a young man who would undertake the care of these mountain people, and be their preacher and friend. The visitor made it quite clear that there was little pay and plenty of hard work attached to this job, but there and then Oberlin felt that it was a call from God to devote his life to the service of these mountain people.

The day came when Oberlin arrived at Waldbach, in the valley among the mountains, where he was to spend the rest of his life. He saw at once that if he was to do any real good as a minister, he must be more than a preacher of sermons; he must attempt to solve other problems that kept his people poverty-stricken and unhappy.

He saw that, with hovels for homes, scrubby and profitless trees for fruit, poor seed for farming, mere trails over the mountains for roads, and minds totally ignorant of what was going on in the world, it would be impossible for him to help his people to become useful servants of Jesus Christ by preaching alone. He saw that soul, body and mind are bound up together in the making of human life, and that where the body does not have a fair chance and the mind does not act, the soul cannot live its full life. In seeing this, Fritz proved his real greatness as a pioneer.

Oberlin set to work at once to establish schools in every village. The people objected to this, fearing that they would have to pay heavy taxes for something they did not want. Some of the unruly men in the neighbourhood went to far as to say: 'Our pastor is too fiery. We will cool him off. We will put him under the pump when he passes by.' Oberlin heard about this threat and at once went to these young men, and said: 'You don't know my horse if you think it possible for you to overtake him. But in order to make it easy for you to carry out your wishes, I will leave my horse at home!' He did so, but was not molested.

At another time he received word that some of his opponents had planned to waylay and beat him. He went immediately to them without fear. 'Here I am, my friends; if I am guilty, punish me for it. It is better that I should deliver myself into your hands than that you should be guilty of an ambuscade to do it.' This sort of cool courage always led to the confusion of his opponents and the abandonment of their hostility.

At last, at great sacrifice on his own part, and the borrowing of money on his own responsibility, the day came when Oberlin saw the walls of his first school building going up. He next proceeded to find and train teachers, and then mapped out lessons for children all the way from the infant school up to those which prepared them for admission to the university. He even used in his schools an idea that is only now finding a place in some of our schools—he gave self-government to the pupils and allowed them to try all cases of bad behaviour that arose. He found that his school system required text-books, and so he set up printing presses and printed the books himself.

He saw that his villagers were shut off from the rest of the world because they had only trails along the sides of the mountains, frequently made impassable by floods. He suggested to his people that this difficulty could be overcome by building a solid road of stone for a mile and a half, with a bridge at the end across one of the mountain gorges. When they heard this, many of his people became certain that he was insane.

Nearly everyone refused to follow him. But one Monday morning, with a pick on his shoulder, and accompanied by three or four who were loyal to him, Oberlin made his way through the village to the mountain-side, and began to build his mile-and-a-half of stone road. The people followed their minister and watched. When they saw him at work, picking, digging and shovelling, there was nothing for them to do but to give in and join him. In the end, a fine road was completed, and the district was connected at last with the outside world.

There was still another serious problem to face. Oberlin found that the farmers knew nothing about how to get the best result from their soil. He therefore proceeded to show them this by cultivating his own land according to improved methods, and with a better grade of seed. His rocky ground was among the worst in the neighbourhood, but he replaced the scrubby, unprofitable fruit trees by improved stock, so that before long his neighbours were standing about admiring and sampling their minister's fruit, convinced that he knew something about their work as well as preaching. He bought improved tools, introduced new methods of taking care of the cattle, and started new industries in the valley.

Suddenly the useful life of Oberlin and his peaceful work in Rock Valley were interrupted in a tragic way. The French Revolution broke out, and the French royal family, the aristocrats, and their supporters were thrown into prison, executed, or fled the country.

One day, the agent of the revolutionaries visited Rock Valley, looking for refugees fleeing from the guillotine. At that very time Oberlin, who could never refuse an appeal for help, was sheltering a daughter of one of the best families of Alsace. Telling the agent to search the house, the pastor fell on to his knees in his study and prayed to God: 'Save this precious life. I see not how it can be done, but Thou canst do it.'

Meanwhile, the agent searched every room until he reached the last bedroom at the top of the house. Here, unaware of her danger, the girl was washing her hands. The agent flung her door open just as she went to get the towel hanging behind the door, which swung back, concealing her. After glancing round the room, the man went downstairs and left the house, while the pastor and his family offered thanks to God for their deliverance.

Several times Oberlin was ordered to Strasbourg to be examined, but was able to satisfy the officials, and for a long time he was almost the only minister of the Gospel not in prison. At last he was arrested and taken to Strasbourg, and it was decided to transport him to Besançon, one of the strongest and worst prisons, when news of the fall of Robespierre from popularity, and his execution by the guillotine, fell like a thunderbolt on the people.

Oberlin was at once released and sent back to his work. By this time the remarkable change wrought in the valley by his labours had made him famous, for the prosperity, happiness and good character of the people in the valley were seen to be the work of their humble pastor. Before he died, Oberlin was awarded the Ribbon of the Legion of Honour, 'on account of the service he has rendered to the State.' But all the old man could say was:

'What have I done to deserve it? Would not anyone in my place have done all that I have done, and more?'

Questions for Discussion.

Why did Oberlin, a minister of the Gospel, build roads and schools and improve the agricultural work of his villagers?

What does Oberlin's story teach us about the extent to which we can serve Jesus Christ?

What was the greatest proof of his usefulness as a servant of Jesus Christ?

How does the life of Oberlin illustrate the parable of the Talents?

IX

GEORGE WHITEFIELD*

PRINCE OF PULPIT ORATORS

ONE would hardly look to the tap-room of an inn for a preacher whose Good News helped to change the heart of the whole nation. Yet George Whitefield, whose name will ever be associated with the Wesleys and the Evangelical Revival of the eighteenth century, was born in the 'Old Bell Inn' at Gloucester, and his early years were spent in the tap-room there.

Thomas Whitefield, the innkeeper, died when George was two years old, so that on his mother fell the burden of carrying on the public-house. As a natural result, the brawls of the rough men who frequented the bar were as familiar to the future preacher as the games he played with other street urchins in the streets of Gloucester. At that time (two hundred years ago), the streets of a town like Gloucester were the only playground and 'school' of the children of the poor. It was in this same cathedral city, not many years afterwards, that Robert Raikes was so dismayed by the profanity, idleness and quarrelsomeness of the neglected children of the poor, that he started the Sunday-school movement on their behalf.†

Young George was a very keen-witted lad, and picked up many things that were not good for him from his mother's tap-room customers. But, because he was so bright, his mother scraped and pinched to send him to

* Based in part on notes by LILIAN E. COX, B.A.

† See the Yarn on ROBERT RAIKES in More Yarns on Social Pioneers.

the Grammar School of St. Mary de Crypt, near by. After the riotous freedom of the streets, young George did not take very kindly to school and its discipline, but tolerated the new order of things because it gave him the opportunity of taking part in the plays which the schoolboys used to perform periodically before the citizens of Gloucester.

Within three years, however, George was tired of school life, and persuaded his mother to let him leave and work as a tapster at the 'Old Bell.' 'I began to assist her in various ways,' Whitefield wrote, years afterwards, 'till at length I put on my blue apron and washed mops, cleaned rooms, and, in a word, became a professed and common drawer (of beer) for nearly a year and a half.'

Young Whitefield was regarded with severe disfavour by the local clergy as a godless young scamp. He had a rare gift of mimicry and would entertain his friends at street corners in mimicking the clergymen reading prayers and even preaching sermons. Yet, beneath the big blue apron of the tavern boy, as he drew ale for the uncouth customers who caroused at his mother's bar, were qualms of conscience, and his mother still clung to the belief that George could do something brilliant if he would.

One day there came to the 'Bell Inn' a young man who spoke of his experiences at Oxford. Mrs. Whitefield listened eagerly, and found he had worked his way through by entering as a servitor, or one who was allowed to study in return for acting as servant to wealthier students. What a chance for a boy like George! She poured out the tale to him, and so enthused him that the youth agreed to go back to school again, work hard at his books, and as soon as he should be ready, try for a servitorship at Oxford. It was not easy for the lad to start lessons again alongside boys much younger than himself, but by now he had caught the vision, and was ready to do anything. So it came about that in 1732, when George was eighteen, he won his servitorship and went up to Oxford. The tapster from the 'Bell Inn' was a student at last.

Among all that George Whitefield learnt at Oxford, one set of experiences stands out. He became converted. The words are easy to write or say, but for Whitefield they meant a very great deal. They meant that life became full of a great and overflowing joy, something which he longed to share with everyone. It set him on the look-out for unfortunate or oppressed men and women who needed help, and made him give up his own ease and comfort to help the wretches in the filthy prison, and the unfortunate women who tried to commit suicide. It meant that he got up at four every morning in order to have time to read the Bible, talk to God, and listen for His guidance. However much the rich and careless young gallants of the university laughed at him, George chose to meet with other undergraduates who felt as he did, and regarded the nickname they earned, 'The Holy Club,' as an honour.

In that Holy Club, George Whitefield met Charles Wesley, and in 1735, when he was twenty-one, Whitefield definitely joined Wesley's 'society,' and determined to give his whole life to the proclaiming of the Good News of Jesus Christ. In June, 1736, when he was twenty-two, Whitefield knelt in the familiar dimness of the cathedral at Gloucester, and was ordained a clergyman (deacon) of the Anglican Church. What must have been his feelings as he stood up on the next Sunday to preach his first sermon in the Church of St. Mary de Crypt? There before him were the schoolboys, in their rows; there were the men and women who had known him as a mischievous boy, or had applauded his efforts as a boy actor; there sat men he had served with beer at the 'Bell Inn.' Many of them had come to listen to him in a spirit of mockery. Soon the laughter faded from their eyes, and many a man came out of church that day declaring that he had never heard such a sermon.

George Whitefield was now set on fire for the Gospel. The glorious truth was burning in his heart, bright and pure; God could redeem any man's life from unhappiness and selfishness and greed, and from all the other ugly things which spoil human life. This good news was for *all*. The clergy of that day were, for the most part, lazy and conventional; in many a parish church the Good News was not proclaimed from year's end to year's end. In the poorest hovels of the land, and in its richest mansions, were those who alike needed to hear the message, alike needed its glorious renewal in their lives.

Not only in England, but across the wide ocean, in the new lands of America, where colonies were being founded and the earliest settlements were not yet a hundred years old, were others who equally needed the message. There, perhaps, the need was even greater; they were in spiritual poverty, and the rich at home in England were their brothers in Christ and ought to help them. O, the greatness of the opportunity!

Young Whitefield, with all the gifts of voice and manner which had made him a star in the school plays, with all the graces of character that he had learned from his Lord and in the fellowship of the Holy Club, threw himself into his great life-work—to preach to *all* the good news, so eloquently and so powerfully that it could not be rejected; and to win the help of the wealthy for the poor and needy overseas.

Few men have had greater power than Whitefield as a preacher. The famous Lord Chesterfield, a polished

man of the world and by no means one to be swept off
his feet, was once in his congregation, when Whitefield
described in his own vivid way the plight of the sinner
as that of a blind beggar stumbling unwittingly nearer
and nearer the edge of a precipice. Lord Chesterfield
was so rapt in his attention that at the final touch he
bounded to his feet with the exclamation, 'Good God,
he's gone.'

The fashionable world of London rallied to Whitefield's
sermons, and called him 'The Boy Preacher.' In a
year or two he was off to Georgia as a missionary, taking
with him the gifts he had collected for the poor in that
colony. But after a few months he returned; he had
conceived the idea of founding a great orphanage for
fatherless children out there, and came home to plead
its cause and collect the necessary funds. For the rest
of his life we find him going backwards and forwards
between the British Isles and Georgia, or touring the
whole of England. On both sides of the Atlantic he
never ceased from his preaching tours, travelling from
place to place, preaching to great crowds in chapels
and meeting-halls and in the open air, winning hundreds
to join him in the service of Jesus Christ, pleading the
cause of his charities with the wealthy, ever thinking out
fresh benefactions, organizing them, raising money for
their support.

He had a message for the lords and ladies of London
society, where his chief patron was Lady Huntingdon.
He went to the rough, wild miners of Kingswood, outside
Bristol—so fierce a gang that the soldiers were called
out against them again and again. He gathered them
in the open air, and spoke to them so that the tears
began to run down their grimed faces and make white
gutters on their cheeks. He travelled north to Scotland;
he crossed the sea to Ireland; he held a mission in

fashionable Bath, and others in the new manufacturing towns that were beginning to spring up. He became nation-famous, as well-known, as well-loved, and as well-hated, as John Wesley, who was working on similar lines at the same time.

Some of the bishops refused him permission to preach in the churches in their dioceses; he replied that he could only offer them 'the dilemma of either allowing my divine commission or of denying your own.' Some of his supporters disapproved of his unconventional ways, and feared lest he was growing too disreputable. 'Preach only to the Lord's people,' they urged. But Whitefield knew the answer to that, and he put it with characteristic vividness: 'The devil's people are in more need of preaching,' he said, and carried on.

Thirteen times he crossed the Atlantic Ocean, and in a ministry of thirty-four years preached nearly eighteen thousand sermons. In England, Scotland, Wales, Ireland, in the West India Islands, and in every colony in America, he preached 'the Word of Life.' No man ever preached to greater crowds. Twenty thousand in Philadelphia, thirty thousand on Boston Common, in Kingswood ten thousand, on Hampton Common twelve thousand, and at Moorfields sixty thousand thronged to hear him.

Whitefield had a fine presence, his personal appearance being much in his favour. He was of medium height, well-proportioned and graceful. His eyes, which spoke volumes, were of a dark blue; but one of them had a slight squint, which gave his revilers a subject for ridicule, for they called him 'Doctor Squintum'—not that he cared.

Whitefield was not only the orator of Nature, but also of art. He studied oratory; he drilled himself; he copied the finest models; he studied to show himself 'a workman that needed not to be ashamed.' Every accent of his voice spoke to the ear; every feature of his face, every gesture, spoke to the eye, so that the most careless found their attention gripped. He was a greater preacher than John Wesley, but lacked Wesley's constructive ability.*

When he was only fifty-six, his friends said that he looked 'an old, old man, fairly worn out.' But he did not stop preaching. He went back to America for the last time in 1770; ill and feeble, he could not go out to preach in a certain town, but the people crowded into the house where he was staying. His message might help some needy soul; so the valiant preacher, ill as he was, left his bed and tottered to the head of the stairs. By the flickering light of his bedroom candle, he talked to them of his Good News. He spoke on and on till at last the candle burned out in his hand. The life of George Whitefield burned out too, for very soon after he died.

To us his life brings the challenge that in the darkest times the Church has the torch which can light men's way, if only she can find valiant torch-bearers; that the light of the Gospel is for all men, high and low, rich and poor; that the farthest places of the world belong to the Kingdom of our God and of His Christ.

Questions for Discussion.

Why did Whitefield join the 'Holy Club'?
Why did people flock to hear him?
What was his Good News?
Why is the Gospel the only power that can really reform a people?

* See Yarn on John Wesley in *Yarns on Christian Pioneers.*

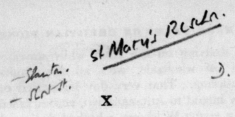

X

DAVID JONES

FOUNDER OF THE CHURCH IN MADAGASCAR

'THERE goes a fine cargo of slaves,' said an Arab dealer, with a grin, to James Hastie, agent of the British Government. Hastie had been standing on the beach at Tamatave, the chief and only port of Madagascar, talking to a young Welshman, and watching a French clipper as it hurried out to sea.

'What!' exclaimed Hastie. 'Were there slaves on board that boat?'

'Rather!' replied the Arab, enjoying the chagrin of the Englishman. 'They were shipped aboard last night while you were being entertained by the captain.'

The British agent looked at the young Welsh missionary, with vexation writ large on his face. They had been waiting for permission from King Radama to go up to the capital of Madagascar to negotiate the end of the slave traffic, and had been cordially entertained by the captain of the French vessel on the previous evening. They had been surprised at his excess of hospitality shown by entertaining them in his cabin till a late hour, spinning travel yarns as only a voluble ship's captain can. Little did they imagine that while they were safely closeted in the wily captain's cabin, a cargo of slaves had been quietly slipped on board, under cover of the darkness, so that the vessel could depart next morning without the interference of this British agent. How thoroughly he had been duped!

This incident made Hastie determine to wait no

59

longer dallying on the coast while slaves were being carried off wholesale, with all the resultant misery and suffering. That very day he started on the long journey inland to Antananarivo, accompanied by David Jones, a young Welshman who had dedicated his life to the conquest of Madagascar for Jesus Christ.

The intrepid travellers endured many trials during the journey by palanquin (a rough litter borne by natives) and dug-out canoe, through forests, across lakes and past clusters of tall-roofed huts where natives came out to stare, because they had never seen white men before.

David Jones was thrilled by his first glimpse of Antananarivo, the capital he had vowed to conquer for Jesus Christ. Built on a long and rocky hill, it was a landmark for miles around. The king received them in a friendly way, and after many days' negotiations, Radama not only signed a treaty abolishing slavery, but opened his capital to the Gospel. Two months later, David Jones opened a little school under royal patronage, but only three children appeared—the people were afraid of the strange white man.

Finding, however, that the three scholars had not been harmed, but had enjoyed going to school, the natives sent more scholars next day, and before long the schoolhouse was crowded to the doors. In two months, sixteen children could read verses from the New Testament, and the king had promised to build a school and a mission house for David Jones. When another Welshman, David Griffiths, arrived a few months later, he found that the work of conquering the capital for Christ had made a good start.

For the next four years, David Jones grappled with the tremendous task of making a written language for the Malagasy people; in the end, it was completed and the work begun of putting the words of the English

Bible into the new language. A red-letter day came when a long line of native bearers from the coast climbed the hill into the capital, carrying big packages on their shoulders. David Jones welcomed them with great joy, for these packages contained parts of a printing-press.

With them came Charles Hovenden, a missionary-printer. But alas for David Jones' hopes, before the packages could be undone, the terrible Malagasy fever had laid hold of the printer, and in a few hours he was dead. For twelve months Jones waited, hoping for the arrival of another printer. At last, in desperation, he vowed that he would find a way somehow of putting the press together, and after many attempts he succeeded. Before long the first sheets of the Malagasy Bible were printed—badly, it is true, for Jones was an amateur printer—but they could be read!

When King Radama died, the rightful heir was killed by one of Radama's wives, who seized the throne and became Queen Ranavalona. David Jones feared the worst, for Ranavalona was an enemy of the Gospel, and a supporter of the old gods of Madagascar. As if to cheer and enhearten him, however, several of the leading men of the capital declared they would henceforth serve Jesus Christ, and one Sunday morning David Jones had the great joy of baptizing twenty-eight Malagasy. Thus, despite all difficulties and obstacles, the Church of Jesus Christ was founded in the capital of heathen Madagascar.

Jones soon found that Queen Ranavalona and the heathen priests were trying to spoil the work of the missionaries in all sorts of quiet ways. The queen, however, did not want to stop the work of the white men while they were teaching her people useful trades, which brought wealth and prestige to the capital. But she vowed that, as soon as her people had learned all that the artisan-missionaries could teach them, out the white men should all go.

One day a tall Malagasy appeared at the mission house door, bearing a message from Ranavalona.

'The queen sends you word that she would like to know whether you can teach her people something useful, such as the making of soap, from the materials in this country. If not, it is her command that you leave the country at once.'

The missionaries looked at each other in dismay.

'How can we teach them soap-making?' said David Jones. 'We don't know the necessary chemical compounds, nor how to obtain them here.'

'The challenge must be accepted,' replied James Cameron, a carpenter-missionary. 'We must find some way of making that soap; otherwise all our work will come to an end.'

So the messenger was sent back to the queen with the assurance that the missionaries' answer would be ready in a week's time.

Then began a week of feverish activity and anxiety for David Jones and his friends. Every day and all day was spent in experimenting in the art of making soap. Suet and fat could be obtained in plenty, but the native equivalents of potash and soda were not such a simple matter. The wood of various kinds of trees was burned, in the hope that the ashes would produce the needed chemicals, without success. Attention was then devoted to burning all kinds of plants, but without avail. Still the experiments went on, and many pounds of good fat were wasted in Cameron's workshop in a nearby village.

At last the queen's messenger appeared, and demanded the promised reply. To the man's amazement, David Jones stepped forward, holding out two small bars of soap.

'Take these to the queen,' he said, 'and tell Her Majesty that these have been made entirely from the products of her country, and that we can teach her people how to make good soap.'

Two bars of soap had saved the mission!

The queen was so delighted with the soap that David Jones had no difficulty in making an agreement with her, under which Cameron was to build a factory and teach a number of Malagasy youths the secrets of soap manufacture. Orders were also secured from the queen for sufficient soap to keep the white men busy for several years.

Thus the evil queen was foiled in her plan to give the missionaries an impossible task, as a pretext for sending them out of the country. And so, while the soap industy was being developed by James Cameron, the work of translating and printing the whole Bible in Malagasy went on unceasingly under the leadership of David Jones.

As time went on, the queen tried to strangle the work of the mission. First she forbade the children to attend the schools; then she restored idolatry, forbade any native to attend the Communion Service, and would not allow any soldier or officer in her army to join the Church or take part in its services. Finally, on 1st March, 1835, the queen called a *kabary* (national assembly); every tribe in the island was summoned to a great plain near the capital. There was a great parade of troops and cannons boomed to terrify the people. Then the chief officers of state appeared, and one of the queen's ministers held up one of her idols and said: 'These are obeyed by Her Majesty the queen, and should be good enough for you.'

Then the queens orator announced a royal decree, ordering all who had become followers of the new religion to report and confess within one month, and that all worship of the new religion and the reading of the Bible must cease, on pain of death.

The *kabary* broke up in great excitement. The Christians went home with heavy hearts, for they had to choose between Christ and the idols of Madagascar.

All the churches and the schools were soon shut, and every Bible that could be found was seized and burnt— and one by one the missionaries had to leave the island. David Jones was the last to go. By staying he only brought more suffering to his Christian friends, for even to speak to him meant arrest and punishment for them. So at last not one white man remained in Madagascar, Christian churches and schools were shut, and old customs and the worship of idols were restored. It looked as though Jesus Christ was defeated, the heathen religion was triumphant, and that all the work of David Jones and others had come to naught.

But the victory of Queen Ranavalona and her native priests was short-lived. They speedily discovered that they had only scattered the Christians, and so had spread the new religion, driving it more deeply into the land. For although the Christians were prevented from meeting for worship, they had not given up following Jesus Christ or reading the Bible. And though some were captured and killed, the majority escaped, wandering in forests and deserts, hiding in caves, suffering privation and hunger, and in some cases starving to death—yet refusing to give up Christ or worship the old gods of their land.

Sometimes they met in caves, and while one mounted guard against the queen's spies, the others prayed, sang hymns, and read the Bible by the light of a tiny lamp, carefully screened lest its flame should betray them. Soldiers and spies of the queen went everywhere, and it seems a miracle that any Christians, or copies of the

Bible, escaped. Beds were examined, rice pits dug over, even the thatch of houses was pulled to pieces in search of Malagasy Bibles, and bonfires were made of all the books that were discovered. Those Christians who were caught, and who refused to forsake Christ, were speared to death or thrown over cliffs. They met death with such courage that the amazed executioners said, 'There must be some magic in this Christian religion, which takes away all fear.'

Once, during the great persecution, David Jones ventured back to Madagascar. He travelled to the capital secretly with a party of traders, but found that he could do nothing to help his friends. During his short stay he saw nine Christians tied under long poles and carried on the shoulders of soldiers to the place of execution.

The death of Ranavalona in 1861 ended the persecution. But, whereas the Christians only numbered 1,000 when the edict forbidding the worship of God was issued in 1835, over 7,000 Christians appeared when freedom to worship God was restored. The might of the tyrant had been powerless over the loyalty of the Christians—the work of David Jones had not failed— Jesus Christ had triumphed gloriously over the forces of evil in Madagascar.

Questions for Discussion.

Why did David Jones persist in his plan to reach the capital?
Why was he so persevering in translating the Bible into Malagasy?
How was the Mission saved by two bars of soap?
What were the forces that were matched when the queen of Madagascar determined to stamp out Christianity? (On her side were the power of government, native priests, national customs, the majority of the people—on the other side were a few Malagasy, eight white missionaries, the Malagasy Bible—and Jesus Christ.)
How were the Christians able to remain loyal?
Why did Christianity triumph?
What does this yarn illustrate in Isaiah 55. 6-11?

XI

FLORENCE NIGHTINGALE

FOUNDER OF MODERN NURSING

ONE day a well-to-do girl, about twelve years old, was riding over the Hampshire Downs on a pony with her vicar. As they went along, the girl saw an old shepherd vainly trying to collect a flock of sheep.

'Where's your dog?' asked the vicar.

'Some boys have thrown stones at him and broken his leg,' was the old shepherd's mournful reply. 'I am afraid I shall have to put the poor animal out of his misery.'

'Can't we do something for him?' said the girl, whose heart was always stirred by suffering. 'You can't do any good, Miss Florence,' said the old shepherd. 'I'll do away with him to-night. That will be the best way to ease his pain.'

But Florence, who loved the dog, was not satisfied. She insisted on going to the shed where the animal was lying, and spent the rest of the day in washing and bandaging the wound, and feeding and caring for the dog. When she reached home that evening, she was soundly scolded for 'wasting her time on a dog.' In spite of that, she insisted on looking after the animal until it fully recovered.

Florence grew up to be a beautiful young woman, refined, well-educated, attractive, but to the disgust of her parents, wanted to become a nurse. In those days there were no trained nurses, and such nursing as was done was the work of ignorant and often drunken

66

women, who were despised as scarcely respectable. Yet, in spite of everything, Florence could not be turned aside from what she felt called by God to do.

While travelling abroad with her parents, she stayed at Kaiserswerth with a German pastor and his wife, and met a deaconess belonging to a school of nursing. A visit to this institution made her long more than ever to become a nurse, but still her parents refused to listen to the bare idea.

Finally, through the help of an aunt, her parents were persuaded to allow her to take charge of what we should call to-day a nursing home for ladies. Here Florence soon showed that she was not only a gentle and clever nurse, but a born healer. But still she was not satisfied. She had dreams of training a new kind of nurse, and sending out to hospitals and to poor districts young women who were trained and capable of helping the sick by gentle and skilful nursing.

Then came her great opportunity. England declared war on Russia, and great battles were fought in the Crimea Peninsula in the Black Sea. Not only were there a great number of wounded British soldiers in the Crimea, but the terrible climate in that part of the world, and the dreadful conditions under which the troops were camped, led to terrible suffering. Hundreds of British soldiers who were wounded or smitten with disease died when their lives could have been saved by proper nursing in a hospital. In those days there was no Red Cross work done in connection with war, the army doctors had no proper hospitals to work in, and the only nursing was done by soldiers. Little wonder, then, that news reached England that the wounded and sick soldiers in the Crimea were dying at a great rate, because the army was without hospital equipment or nurses. Public opinion was aroused; people demanded that the soldiers who were fighting for their country should be properly looked after.

Meanwhile, Florence Nightingale, the woman who had chosen nursing as her life-work, had not been idle. She got together thirty-four trained nurses like herself, who were ready to go out to the Crimea and look after the wounded soldiers. When her plans were ready, she wrote to the Minister of War, offering her services. Two days later she was on her way to the Crimea with thirty-four nurses, the first women from England to go out during war-time to care for the wounded.

On the way out, Florence carefully prepared her plans, well knowing that she had in front of her one of the biggest and most difficult pieces of work ever undertaken by a woman. She arrived at Scutari, where a large barracks belonging to the Turks had been handed over to the English for a hospital. When Florence went inside, her heart sank with dismay. There was no fresh air, no proper drains, no linen sheets, no clean bedding. On the contrary, everywhere was filth, overcrowding and neglect. As soon as she examined the situation, Florence was filled with indignation—she could forgive the muddle and the overcrowding, but not the shocking neglect of the wounded and dying that she saw on all sides.

The first things Florence sent for were two hundred hard scrubbers and sacking for washing the floors. Next, she took over a big Turkish house near by, had boilers put in, and employed soldiers' wives to do the washing for the hospital. Extra kitchens were set up, so that the wounded men could be fed properly. Even this beginning of bringing order out of chaos was only made after this frail and delicate-looking woman of thirty had pleaded, scolded and stormed at the army officers who said that the things she wanted could not be done. 'They must be done,' she said, stamping her foot in vexation; and by brushing aside army regulations and everything that stood in her way, she gradually made the barrack hospital an entirely different place.

The greatest need was medical stores of all kinds, but often when these arrived from England they were locked into storerooms until they had been sorted out and inspected by the proper official.

When Florence Nightingale discovered that the food and medicine she wanted were on the spot, but could not be served out, she said they *must* be served out. Defying all authority and all army orders, she insisted on the stores being opened and the medicines, etc., handed over for the relief of suffering.

In grappling with the tremendous task of turning the filthy and overcrowded barracks into a clean and orderly hospital, Florence's first care was the wounded men who had been so badly neglected. She wore herself out in nursing them back to health and strength. There were four miles of beds when the hospital was properly organised, with scarcely room between them to walk. Yet every night, before she went to rest, Florence Nightingale, lighting her little lamp, went through every ward to see for herself that the wounded and sick men were comfortable for the night.

As she continued her rounds, peace seemed to settle wherever she went. The very sight of her slender form gliding quietly along the corridor brought comfort and hope to many a sufferer. The rough soldiers called her the Lady of the Lamp, and out of love and gratitude for her care, kissed her shadow as it fell across their pillows. She became a fairy godmother to hundreds of soldiers in the barrack hospital. In those days chloroform had not been discovered, and to help men to bear the pain of serious operations, Florence Nightingale went with them into the operating room and stood by to help and soothe them by her presence. Soon all England was ringing with her name, as wounded soldiers wrote home full of praise and thanks for the work of the Lady of the Lamp.

'Before she came, there was cursing and swearing, but afterwards it was as holy as a church.' 'What a comfort it was to see her pass even.' 'She was full of life and fun, especially if a man was a bit downhearted.'

These were some of the things that soldiers wrote home about her in their letters. Long before the war was over, worn out by her work, she succumbed to the Crimean fever, and for days her life was despaired of. Then slowly she recovered, and, although urged by the doctors to sail at once to England to regain her health, she went back to Scutari instead, where she remained until the last wounded soldier had sailed for home.

In the hour of victory, the work of Florence Nightingale was not forgotten, but she refused any reward or honour for her work, and when gifts poured in she used them for founding a training institution for nurses. 'She belongs to the sect of the Good Samaritan,' said an Irish clergyman one day, when the orthodoxy of Florence Nightingale was being questioned. 'I have simply done my Master's work,' she herself said.

Questions for Discussion.

What made Florence Nightingale persist in studying nursing against her parents' wishes?

What gave her an opportunity to become the pioneer of modern nursing?

Why did her task at Scutari demand determination and perseverance, as well as skill and pity?

How did she win the hearts of the wounded soldiers of the Crimea?

Why did she say she only did her Master's work?

How does her story illustrate Luke 10. 25–37?

The Woman who bothered.

XII

MARY REED

WHO WENT TO LIVE AMONG LEPERS

'I HAVE been called by God to come and help you.'

These words were uttered about fifty years ago to a group of lepers, who lived in mud huts perched high on the slopes of the Himalayas in India. They came from the lips of an approaching white woman, and were startling in the extreme. No one of their own race—let alone a white woman—had ever made friendly overtures to them.

The little group was soon joined by other lepers, and before long the white woman, Mary Reed, was holding a short service and explaining her plans for helping them. Tears coursed down the cheeks of many of the sufferers. For the first time since they had been smitten by the terrible disease and so had become helpless outcasts, they heard kind words addressed to them. Mary Reed's promises of help seemed strange and almost unnatural. It is difficult to imagine what her action meant to the outcast lepers, who were believed to be suffering for some terrible sin, and to be without any hope from life or relief through death.

* * *

Years before, when quite a young girl, Mary had devoted her life to Christ's service. She had heard an inner voice calling to her to go to the aid of the women and children shut up in the zenanas, or women's quarters, of India. For eight years she worked in Cawnpore under most trying conditions—in the hot streets and closed apartments—among the women and girls of the stifling Indian city. At last, worn out with this work, she had been sent up into the Himalayas to rest and recover her health in the cooler air of the highlands.

It was while she was staying in the hills that Mary Reed made the distressing discovery that, in that district alone, there were five hundred miserable leper outcasts living in poverty, neglect, and despair, and dead to all ordinary life.

After her brief holiday was finished, Mary Reed returned to Cawnpore to her work, but she could not forget the lepers she had seen in the mountains. Then, twelve months later, her health was so broken that she was sent home to America for special treatment.

In spite of everything that could be done at home, however, Mary Reed's health did not improve, and the doctors failed to understand a tingling pain in her forefinger and a strange spot which had appeared on her face. Then, one day, like a sudden ray of light, Mary Reed guessed that her disease was leprosy! The terrible shock that this realisation first brought with it was followed almost immediately by a great joy as she remembered the Indian lepers. Here was a new work to which God had called her, for she saw at once that as a leper she could go and help the lepers! At first only the doctors knew her secret, for she dared not tell her parents, and had to leave home without special farewells to her relations and friends.

As we have seen above, when Mary Reed reached Chandag once more, she bravely and cheerfully faced the lepers and told them her story, determined to settle down to the work of serving and helping them.

At first, she found her new sphere of life hard and unpleasant. The lepers were horribly disfigured in body, and degraded in their habits by years of cruelty, neglect and suffering. She was handicapped for want of accommodation, for the first leper home she opened was only a few broken-down huts, where thirty-seven lepers lived. Many of them were bad cases, requiring constant attention, and Mary was always at work washing and binding up wounds, and speaking kindly words of comfort and cheer. At the same time, she was herself suffering intense pain, as her own leprosy grew worse. The number of lepers applying for admission to the asylum steadily increased as her patients enjoyed a new lease of life and new joy through her care and teaching.

Sometimes the work was made harder by the quarrels among the lepers, but gradually the kindness and love and quiet power of Mary helped them to learn a new way of life. In particular, the lepers loved Sunday on the Chandag heights, when they gathered in Mary's garden to praise and worship God in one of the loveliest spots on earth. Behind them were the Himalayan peaks, capped with snow, and lit up with a halo of glory by the sunshine. In front stretched the lovely valley of Shor, dotted with villages and clumps of trees, and terraced fields of rice and wheat, with the little river winding in and out like a silver ribbon across the landscape. Before Mary had come to them, the lepers had been dead to the beauty of the world; but now they sang their praises to God for His House of Love perched on the edge of the mountain slopes.

It was not long before the Leper Asylum at Chandag grew far too large for the few rough cottages and small piece of farm land which had at first supported it, so Mary Reed had to set to work busily planning out how to get more land and build new and larger cottages. Unfortunately, trouble arose with the neighbouring villagers, who were puzzled that Mary should take such care and interest in outcast lepers. They made objections because the water for the needs of the asylum was taken from the stream that flowed through their village.

Here was a problem indeed, for Mary had no water on the premises. To add to her difficulties, there was no wall to protect the garden and fowl-house, so that jackals and porcupines destroyed the vegetables and carried off the chickens and eggs.

At last, after no little trouble, a new piece of land was secured, and then began an eager search for a spring or a likely place for sinking a well. A possible spot was found where there was a bed of rocks, but unfortunately Mary was unable to get the digging done to tap the water. A further search for water was therefore started, and finally a good spring was found on a piece of waste land half a mile away in a deep ravine.

After gaining the necessary permission, Mary joyfully made plans to bring the water round the brow of the hill by means of troughs and ditches into the asylum grounds. Many busy weeks were spent in securing labour to do this work, Mary acting as her own works'-foreman. Then came the tremendous task of planning and superintending the erection of the new buildings to hold more lepers, including a hospital for the worst cases, a dispensary for giving out medicine, and a church where the lepers could worship. Then a new village for men and boys was started some distance away. Thus the work grew and extended, and at the end of the third year, seven new buildings were finished, three more were being put up, and four were to be started the following year, so as to make room for eighty lepers to live in comfort.

Then Mary Reed packed her bag and tent, and started off on a long journey to a distant village by the river, where a big heathen festival was being held, in order to tell the Good News of Christ there, and bring back more sufferers to be cared for in the enlarged home for lepers. But she returned home very downcast, as only four lepers had consented to come, the others being kept away by the native priests. Yet she had much joy in her work, for the number of lepers who became Christians was increasing, and, above all, her own health became much better.

'The good hand of the Lord is upon me, and I am not afraid of what the future will bring,' she said to her friends.

Among Mary's large family of lepers were many children who had been driven away from home because of leprosy. Lovingly she cared for them, and in some cases the disease was arrested.

One girl of thirteen had been married at eleven, and then leprosy appeared. She was driven out of the house by her husband and his mother, and was given a corner of the cowshed to sleep and eat in. She was made to work in the fields all day, and finally, being driven away altogether, was found wandering alone by Mary, who brought her into the leper home. The girl became a Christian, and was so happy that she felt glad she was a leper because it had brought her to Mary.

Mary Reed describes one day's work thus:

'For one hour after breakfast, giving directions and superintending putting concrete floor in new hospital, next hour, examined six boys in Hindi—next, received call from distant villagers wanting school opened in their village—another hour superintending builders in hospital and making up accounts—call from native preacher with report of his work—another hour with carpenters—then training leper woman to wash and bathe new leper—gave clothing for new patient—out into fields to look after people cutting hay—returned home to do housework. After lunch, gave medicine to cook's son—another hour with carpenters—off to see lame woman in distant village wanting admittance (found not a leper at all)—rang bell and called lepers for service in chapel, took service—walked half-mile at sunset, then home to write report!'

Little wonder that Mary Reed was too busy to worry about her own health—and in some marvellous way the progress of the disease was arrested.

She served the lepers so well that they all loved her and called her 'Mama.' On her birthday they decorated the verandah of her house with flowers at dawn, and awakened her by their singing. When Mary got out of bed and peeped out, she saw four Bible women and another leper standing there with lights, singing in honour of her birthday, the verandah made beautiful with flowers.

Year after year Mary Reed always stuck to her work, and God wonderfully preserved her life and health. Although living apart from ordinary folk, she was always so jolly that a visitor to the Chandag Asylum once said:

'Miss Reed is so very bright and sane in her outlook, and so keen on her work, that it is an inspiration to meet her; her bright, sunny smile is something to remember.'

In October, 1941, Mary Reed celebrated her jubilee at Chandag, amid great rejoicing among her fellow-workers and all the patients.

The hopeless and homeless outcast beggars are now bright and happy, living in comfortable homes and joyfully joining in God's worship in their own beautiful church—literally they have been brought out of death into life. And although Mary Reed passed to her reward in 1943 the work still goes on.

Questions for Discussion.

Why did Mary Reed offer to befriend the lepers?
Why did she rejoice when she discovered she was a leper?
How has she been able to serve the lepers of India?
How does her life illustrate the benefits of the Gospel, summed up in Matthew 11. 5?

XIII

VERNON HAROLD STARR

THE BELOVED PHYSICIAN OF PESHAWAR

ONE day, Dr. Pennell, the well-known medical missionary, whose work on the Indian Frontier was described as 'worth a couple of regiments to the British any day,' went to Oxford to talk about his work. Among the audience was a boy of fifteen, working in a chemist's shop. This lad was thrilled by the stories told by Pennell of doctoring the wild Afghans on the Indian Frontier. As a result, Pennell seemed a great hero in his eyes, and one remark made by the doctor stuck in his memory ever afterward: 'The finest thing in the world is the Medical Missionary.'

The chemist's assistant went back to his work with new ideas of life and its purposes. Two years later, he wrote in his diary, 'I am almost decided to be a medical missionary—Vernon Harold Starr.'

Soon after this, young Starr went to a Missionary Exhibition that was being held in Oxford, and that decided it. His ambition was not easy to realise at nineteen, when he had finished his apprenticeship to the chemist, for he was too poor to study medicine to become a doctor, so had to go on working as a chemist, studying medicine in his spare time and putting his whole heart into it. Two years later, Starr gained his reward, winning a medical scholarship in London.

For the next five years he worked hard as a medical student at King's College Hospital, teaching every Sunday in a poor school at Islington, and devoting his holidays at the seaside to mission work among the boys and girls. Whatever he did, he worked so hard at it with such white-hot enthusiasm, that the other students chaffed him and said his initials 'V.H.S.' stood for 'Very Hot Stuff.' Starr only laughed at their ridicule, and was always so jolly and smiling that they also called him 'Twinkle, Twinkle.' When Starr won his doctor's degree, he became House Surgeon in a Devonshire hospital in order to gain experience, and was such a favourite with the children that they called him 'the little doctor with the curly hair.'

At last Dr. Starr realised his great ambition, and sailed for India.

'Now begins my life work,' he entered in his diary. When he reached the Mission Hospital at Peshawar, he found plenty of work to do. The hospital stood just inside the Indian Frontier, near the famous Khyber Pass, and on the road into Afghanistan. His patients were nearly all Pathans—the fierce and wild hillmen of the Indian Frontier.

The little white-coated doctor, with his curly hair and merry smile, plunged into his work with a right goodwill. Sometimes a fierce-looking warrior was brought in suffering from a terrible gunshot wound, eager to be healed for the sole purpose of going out to get his revenge on his enemy. Often men and women and little children were covered with sores that had been made worse because a mullah (native priest) had given them filthy mud, which he called 'holy earth,' to rub into the sore for a cure. Thus the superstition and ignorance of the natives made Dr. Starr's work both difficult and trying.

One morning, he went into the hospital and to the bedside of a man whose wound he had carefully dressed on the previous day. Imagine his surprise to find no

trace of the bandage, and the wound exposed to full view.
'Where is the bandage?' he demanded. A relative
sitting beside the bed pointed to the man's filthy turban,
and unrolling it, the doctor found the bandage carefully
stowed away inside it. 'Sahib, I only wanted to look
at it,' the man whined, as the doctor patiently began
dressing the wound over again.

On another occasion he found that the family of a
man with a broken arm had taken off the splint and
rubbed salt and butter into the fracture 'to put it right.'
Such tricks were the more vexing because there were
always twice as many people to be doctored than the
hospital could attend to, and the demand made upon
the skill, time, nerves and patience of the doctor was
tremendous. There was only one other doctor at the
hospital, and once between them they performed 129
operations in one day, working from sunrise to dusk.
Yet Dr. Starr was never too busy to find time to teach the
patients about Jesus Christ, nor to take his turn at conducting the worship in the mission church to which the
hospital was attached, and to be a friend to all who needed
his help.

In 1914, when war broke out in Europe, Dr. Starr
was placed in charge of the hospital, with its 100 beds,
and had the care of all the mission work on his shoulders
as well as all the doctoring. With his good-humoured
smile, he grappled with the task with undismayed
enthusiasm. Many of the people who came for treatment had diseased eyes, and had travelled hundreds
of miles because the fame of the white doctor, who
could give them new eyes, had reached them in their
distant homes. Often through dirt and neglect their
sight had gone for ever, but in some cases he was able
to restore their sight and send them home delighted,
not only with their new eyes, but with the story of Jesus

Christ, Who had healed the blind and 'Who went about doing good.'

Often, however, the superstition of the people hindered his work. One man removed the bandage from his eyes the day after his operation, in order to put some 'holy earth,' which he had brought from a local shrine, into his eyes, in case the doctor's work had not been successful. Thus it was often very discouraging, but the little doctor had no thought of giving up—he had come out to serve the people of India at the command of his Master, Jesus Christ, and that was sufficient. He accepted their ignorance and their passion for fighting as a challenge to teach them the law of love of his Master, and plodded on in face of all discouragement. Every day brought fresh cases, and his work of healing seemed as fruitless as trying to keep the sea from advancing when the tide was coming in.

One day a girl was brought to the out-patients' department with her arm and shoulder shattered by a gunshot. 'It was the work of my enemy,' the girl's father told him, in a matter-of-fact way; 'he could not shoot me, so he shot my daughter.'

One day Starr wrote in his diary, 'Nearly 400 out-patients to-day, certainly work enough for all—a bit tired.' No wonder he was tired. A furlough in England was long overdue, but because there was so much work to do, and it was war-time, and there was no one else to do it, he went on serving the people.

Every night the doctor went to his bed dog-tired with the day's work; but even then he could not always rest, for accidents or blood-feuds brought people knocking at his door for immediate attention at all hours of the night. Nevertheless he was always cheerful and ready to help. When others were surprised at his cheerfulness and patience, he would gently remind them that he was a disciple of Jesus Christ, who had often been tired because

sufferers came to Him for healing in such numbers that
He could not get time to eat or drink.

'He was always ready for another service by day and
night, our Doctor Sahib—he runs to do it,' the natives said.

An army officer who visited Peshawar was amazed
and thrilled at what he saw. 'It was endless work from
early morning till late at night. Single-handed, owing
to the war, Dr. Starr had to treat all the medical and
surgical cases himself, do all the major operations,
supervise the half-trained native helpers, maintain discipline, pay wages, keep accounts, write records and bear
all the anxiety and responsibility of the place and more
—for he never allowed his work for the body to obscure
his work for the soul; public prayers before the morning's
work, a short prayer before a serious operation, and
on Sundays, a sermon to help at the church at Peshawar
or some outlying station. Always overworked, always
tired, yet always cheerful, he gave up all he had.'

The thing that gave the doctor the greatest joy was when
one of the patients, or one of his native helpers, followed
Starr's example and became a follower of Jesus Christ.

One day, an Afridi boy came to Peshawar Hospital
and asked for work, and was taken in as a coolie. He
proved a very willing and good worker, and soon, to
Dr. Starr's great joy, wanted to become a Christian,
so was baptized. Soon afterwards his father and other
members of the clan came to Peshawar and persuaded
the boy to ask for 'time off to visit a sick relative just
over the border.' The boy went, but did not come
back. A long while after, Dr. Starr heard that the boy
had been decoyed home in this way, and then ordered
to recant his Christianity or be killed, and had chosen
to become a martyr for Christ.

The boy's family held Dr. Starr responsible for his
death, and vowed to take blood-revenge.

Four years later, three men, believe to be relatives of this boy, came to the hospital in the dead of night and knocked at the door. Always ready to serve, the doctor got up from his bed and went to the door to see who needed his help. 'What is it?' he asked, peering into the darkness. There was a swift movement from without, a loud cry rang out on the night air, and the doctor staggered back into the room, calling out, 'I am stabbed.' His wife rushed to his help, the alarm was sounded, and everything done to save the life of their beloved doctor, but in the late afternoon of the following day he died. He was buried amidst a great throng, English and Indians vying with each other to show their love for the little doctor who had laid down his life in his Master's service.

'That was no funeral,' said an English soldier, thinking of the note of triumph that had marked the day. 'Look! Eternal Life!' an Indian said, pointing to the dead man, whose influence would never die amongst them. 'They have not killed him, but they have killed thousands of us,' said another Indian, whose life had been restored by the doctor's kind skill.

'Had I known I would have given my life instead of his,' said another. So they sang a glorious Easter hymn of the victory of life over death as they laid his body in the grave, feeling that his spirit was still with them. And on the cross that marked his grave, they carved the motto of his life: 'For to me to live is Christ, and to die is gain.'

Questions for Discussion.

What made young Starr want to be a medical missionary?
Why did he go out to India?
What made his work so difficult at Peshawar?
Why did he teach his patients about Jesus?
How much did he give in the service of India and Jesus Christ?
What does his story suggest to us?

NOTES FOR TEACHERS AND LEADERS

AT the suggestion of fellow-workers, I have made the Yarns in this book shorter than some of those in earlier books in this series: most of them can be told to a group of adolescents in about twenty minutes. This abbreviation of the original Yarns has made it possible to include a greater variety and number of characters in the book, which is an obvious advantage. Of set purpose, also, the subjects of the Yarns are varied.

The following notes are intended to provide further information for the teacher, to enable him (or her) to answer questions and supplement the facts given in the Yarn itself.

I—IGNATIUS

Aim of the Yarn.

To show how Ignatius's loyalty to Christ even unto death, proved an inspiration to others to remain loyal, and is an example to us.

Biographical.

The early days, and most of the details of the life of Ignatius are lost in oblivion. He was reputed to be a native of Antioch in Syria, converted by the Apostle John. In A.D. 69, when Bishop Evodius died, Ignatius was appointed as his successor. When the Emperor Trajan halted at Antioch on his expedition against the Parthians in A.D. 114, a fresh wave of persecution broke out, and Ignatius, instead of waiting to be hunted out and arrested, went boldly to the Emperor, as described in the Yarn. He faced the trials and dangers on the journey to Rome without fear or complaint, and was finally thrown to the lions in the arena at Rome. He is said to be the author of several valuable epistles. 'Zeal for martyrdom in the later days became a disease in the Church, but in the case of Ignatius it is the mark of a hero.'—*Encyclopædia Britannica*.

II—TELEMACHUS

Aim of the Yarn.

To show how the action of an unknown man challenged the people of Rome to apply a Christian standard to their amusements, and to discover a new value for human life.

Historical.

In spite of the fact that the Christian Church gained recognition in A.D. 313 and the Emperors of Rome after Constantine (except for Julian) were Christians in name, the usual games and shows went on in the Colosseum. The celebration of victories in war were still the occasion for them. When Stilicho, who commanded the armies of the West for the boy-emperor Honorius, defeated the Goths at Polentia on Easter Day, A.D. 403, and so saved Italy, the Senate invited him to celebrate it with a triumph. The old-time ceremonies were performed, except that the Christian churches were visited instead of the heathen temples. The same games were held as before, and combats to the death were arranged between the gladiators. But on this occasion, the latter were interrupted in the name of God by the hermit, Telemachus. Then only did 'Christian' Rome see the implications of its own official creed.

Biographical.

Of Telemachus little is known to history, beyond that he came from the East. Tennyson in his poem sees in the monk's early asceticism and retirement from the world the natural preparation for his heroic sacrifice to raise the standard of value of human life. Gibbon, referring to Telemachus's death, indulges in a character- istic gibe, that 'his death was more useful to mankind than his life,' and described him as 'the only monk who ever died a martyr to humanity.' In the Yarn, an imagined form has been given to the call which came to him in his distant hermitage; quotations are used from Tennyson's poem.

Reference Books.

A Book of Golden Deeds, by C. Yonge; *St. Telemachus*, by Tennyson.

III—AUGUSTINE OF HIPPO

Aim of the Yarn.

To show how Augustine found peace, joy and his life-work by forsaking selfish pleasure for the service of Jesus Christ.

Historical.

Augustine of Hippo* lived from A.D. 354–430, so that his life covers the period of the downfall of the Roman Empire in the West. The background of his life was, therefore, anything but peaceful. In the year that he was born, Gallus was being entrapped and put to death at Pola, and Julian the Apostate imprisoned at Milan. When he began to study at Carthage, the Huns were breaking into Russia. He reached Milan when Ambrose was in the midst of his great controversy with Justina. The sack of Rome by Alaric the Goth was the most striking event of his later life, and at the time he died the Vandals were over-running the Roman province in Africa, and besieging Hippo, the town of which he was bishop.

* So called to distinguish him from Augustine of Canterbury.

Biographical.

Aurelius Augustinas was born at Tagaste (Tajelt) in Numidia, North Africa, on 13th November, 354. His father, Patricius, was a burgess in limited circumstances, genial, hot-tempered, licentious. His mother, Monica, was a Christian of rare piety and devotion, whose prayers and devoted efforts were successful at last in bringing both her husband and son into the Christian faith. Although from his earliest days Monica sought to instruct her son in the faith and love of Jesus Christ, she appeared to make no real impression upon his youthful mind, and his young manhood was spent in indulgence and sensuality. He studied at Madaura, Carthage and Rome. He reached Milan at the age of thirty, at the time when Ambrose, the famous preacher, was bishop. His conversion was as sudden and dramatic as that of St. Paul. He resigned his professorship of rhetoric, was baptized by Ambrose, and returned to Africa, where he lived in religious retirement for several years. He then went to Hippo to visit a friend, and by seeming accident was chosen as presbyter. Finally, he became sole bishop of Hippo—a post he occupied with unique distinction until his death in 430. His learning and great gifts marked him out as the foremost leader of religious controversy of his age, and his influence on the Christian Church has probably been greater than any other individual since his day.

IV—ANSKAR

Aim of the Yarn.

To show that the spread of the Gospel in Europe was due to the heroic persistence of little-known pioneers like Anskar.

Historical.

The Mohammedan religion was at the zenith of its power in Europe towards the close of the seventh century. It swept westward over Africa, Spain and Southern Gaul, but Europe was saved by the great victory of the Franks at Tours under Charles Martel, in 732. Soon afterwards, the Franks were Christianized by missionaries from Rome and England, and the Pope made Charles Martel king of the Franks. Later on, his son, Pepin, conquered the German nation, partly to aid Boniface, an English monk, who had gone there as a missionary. Pepin's policy was either to Christianize or kill the Germans, but against this Alcuin, another English missionary, protested. In the reign of the famous Charlemagne, Pepin's son, the Teutonic and Latin races were largely united, and culture and law were so developed that Charlemagne has been called 'the Moses of the Middle Ages,' His successor, Louis the Pious, encouraged the spread of the Gospel among the heathen, and the Christian faith was thus spread to the north and east. It was in this work that Anskar was prominent.

Biographical.

Anskar (also called Ansgar and Ansgarius), was born in 801 at Corbei, near Amiens, Picardy, of noble parents, and dedicated from birth to the service of God. He was educated at the Abbey of Corbei, one of the best monastic institutions in that part of the Empire. As the result of visions, he felt called to take the Gospel to the heathen, and was chosen by Louis the Pious to take the Gospel to Jutland about 826. In 829 he was sent to Sweden with the Gospel, and in time he became known as 'the Apostle of the North,' was made Archbishop of Hamburg by King Louis in 831, the appointment being confirmed by the Pope soon afterwards. Anskar died, full of years and honour, at Bremen in 865.

V—JOHN HUSS

Aim of the Yarn.

To show how, through studying the Bible and the teaching of Wycliffe, John Huss started a crusade of reform and became one of the founders of Protestantism.

Historical.

The Reformation in Bohemia began before the days of John Huss, since he had three reforming predecessors : Conrad of Waldhausen, Milic of Moravia, Matthias of Janow, a Bohemian noble. Partly due to the work of these men in the first half of the 14th century, religion in Bohemia reached a higher level than in other places, and the ground was prepared for the preaching of Huss in the first part of the 15th century. Meanwhile, John Wycliffe had laid the foundations of the Protestant Reformation by his writing, preaching and Bible translation in England from 1350 to 1384. John Huss, who was fifteen years old when Wycliffe died, drew much of his inspiration for his reforming work in Bohemia from Wycliffe's writings, and started the Hussite movement, which had not spent itself before the reforming zeal flamed out again, this time in Florence, where Savonarola was its champion. It remained for Tyndale in England, Martin Luther in Germany, and John Calvin in Switzerland, to carry on the reforming work, and firmly establish the Protestant Reformation in the 15th century.

The depths to which the Christian Church had sunk at this time is indicated by the fact that there were three rival Popes, all warring with each other, each having his own party among the prelates and clergy, and each cursing the other as anti-Christ. The prelates and the clergy lived notoriously evil lives, and showed the way in villainy to the people. The Church was a centre of darkness rather than light, and the mass of the people were left without any religious teaching whatsoever. To say this is not to forget the fact that in every land there were a few devout and earnest clergy who deplored the evil example of their colleagues, and prayed and worked for a brighter day.

Biographical.

John Huss (born 1373, died 1415) was the son of poor parents living at Husinetz in South Bohemia. He entered the clerical profession and became a priest when twenty-five, lecturing at Prague University. In 1402 he became preacher at Bethlehem Chapel in Prague. Soon afterwards he began reading the works of Wycliffe, and as a result he became notorious for his outspoken preaching against the sins of the clergy and the shortcomings of the Church. He completely won the hearts of the common people, and was elected Rector of the University in 1409. He was now charged with heritical teaching and, proving recalcitrant, was excommunicated in 1410. This led to popular riots in his favour, with the result that the city was placed under a Papal interdict in 1411. Huss was summoned to appear before the Council of Constance on a charge of heresy, and being promised a safe-conduct by the Emperor Sigismund, went to Constance in November, 1414. In violation of this promise of safe-conduct, he was thrown into prison, and after several trials in which he obtained no fair hearing, the case being settled beforehand against him, he was burnt at the stake on 6th July, 1415.

VI—HUGH LATIMER

Aim of the Yarn.

To show how Latimer devoted his life and, in the end, sacrificed it, for Christian truth and an open Bible.

Historical.

The background of Latimer's life and work is the England of 1500 to 1556. The century opened with an event which was more significant than the crushing of pretenders to Henry VIII's throne—the arrival of Colet and Erasmus in England, fired with the love of the New Learning, which had come to Europe through the fall of Constantinople. Men were now able to read the New Testament in its original language for the first time, and this, with the works of the Greek philosophers, turned men's minds to newer ways of thought. Colet and Erasmus both found in the New Testament the ground for a plea for a religion without image-worship or the adoration of saints, and they aimed at getting the living picture of the Jesus of the Gospels known to men. The New Learning had powerful friends : Fisher, bishop of Rochester, Foxe, bishop of Winchester, and Archbishop Warham. Schools were established, like Colet's at St. Paul's, all over the country.

Side by side with the New Learning went the development of

the power of the monarchy, under the administration of Cardinal Wolsey and Thomas Cromwell. The climax of this development came when, through the Roman Church refusing to sanction Henry's divorce, the king cut the knot by becoming Supreme Head of the Church of England. This was an impossible situation for men like More, and he paid a full price for his refusal to acknowledge the king as supreme. Some of the divines of England who sided with the divorce policy were also leaning towards the criticism of the Church due to their 'new learning.' These were often in danger of being charged with heresy by those who supported the old ideas as to the Church's place and power, but because of the side they had taken over the king's divorce they found a friend in Cromwell. The events on the Continent and the translation of the Bible in England gave an impetus towards the Protestant position; the religious houses were suppressed under Cromwell, and some of the bishops were prepared to deny the doctrine of transubstantiation. The reign of Edward VI saw rapid changes towards the Protestant position. The service of the Church was conducted in English, altars of stone were destroyed and replaced by tables placed in the centre of the church. Forty-two articles of religion (thirty-nine of which still remain) were introduced, and stated the formal doctrine of the Church of England. The accession of Mary changed all this again; the old Romish forms were soon restored, and those who had been leaders in the Reform movement were imprisoned and sent to death at the stake, among them Hugh Latimer and his friend, Nicholas Ridley. These, with many humble men and women, lighted the candle of Protestant truth which has never been put out.

Biographical.

Hugh Latimer (born 1490, died 1555), was the popular preacher of the Reformation. He won fame by his fiery moral earnestness and the direct and homely speech of his sermons. He was sharp in his judgments and condemnation of those who opposed him. For his own decided opinions about the reform of the abuses of Church practices and belief he was often in trouble. He gave full support to Henry's Act of Supremacy, and was made Bishop of Worcester in 1535. He supported the popular demand for the suppression of image-worship and sent the statue of the Virgin in his cathedral to London to be burned with others. The zeal of many of the reformers outran their discretion, and to stop the scene of ribaldry at the celebration of the Mass the Six Articles Law was passed in 1539, but as Latimer could not subscribe to this, he resigned his see and was arrested. His life was saved by the power of Cromwell, but for a few years there is no record of his activities.

'In April, 1554, he was examined at Oxford, and committed to Bocardo, the common gaol there, where he lay for more than a twelve-month, feeble, sickly, worn-out with his hardships. In

September, 1555, with Ridley and Cranmer he was brought before a commission, and after an ignominious trial, was found guilty of heresy and handed over to the secular power. On the 16th of October he was burned with Ridley opposite Balliol College. Latimer's character presents a combination of many noble and disinterested qualities. He was brave, honest, devoted and energetic, homely and popular, yet free of all violence; a martyr and hero, yet a plain, simple-minded, unpretentious man. Humour and earnestness, manly sense and direct evangelical fervour distinguish his sermons and his life, and make them alike interesting and admirable.'—*Chambers's Encyc.*

Reference Books.

Somervell's *Short History of Our Religion* (Geo. Bell, 6s.); Demaus' *Hugh Latimer* (from a library).

VII—VINCENT DE PAUL

Aim of the Yarn.

To show that serving Jesus Christ means helping all sorts of poor and needy people in everyday life.

Biographical.

Vincent de Paul was born in 1576, near Dax, in Gascony, not far from the Pyrénées. His father was a poor villager, an openhearted peasant who brought up his children in the love of God. Vincent, his fourth child, early showed himself different from the rest, and wished so earnestly to be a priest that his father sent him to school to the Franciscan Friars, and afterwards to the University of Toulouse. A few years later he was returning from Marseilles to Larbonne when an Algerian brigantine swept down and captured the barque, and he and his shipmates were taken captives to Tunis, with the result recorded above.

Vincent was sold to a fisherman first and then to a chemist, and later on to a farmer, who was a renegade Christian with three wives. Vincent was the means of showing a new faith tò one of the wives who spoke to her husband, in wonder that he should have deserted so beautiful a creed. The farmer remembered his Christian childhood and fled with Vincent, who settled at Clichy, and was untiring in his labours amongst the poor and the sick; he taught the children and drew all hearts to him through his strong personal attraction. Later he became tutor to the family of a French nobleman, but the longing in his heart to devote himself to the poor was so great that in 1617 he ran away.

Eventually Vincent went to Marseilles to investigate the condition of the convicts, and found it most deplorable. He threw himself into the task of helping them, and his gentle disposition and marvellous goodness soon produced effect. The investigation of their

condition made him alive to many other miserable social conditions
of his day. Begging and vagabondage were rife in many parts and
both beggars and the deserving poor were neglected. In one city
he organised a sort of voluntary poor rate and arranged for the
relief of the really needy. He organised much benevolent work
in Paris, and died, full of good works, in 1660, and left an example
of simple Christian goodness that belongs to the Church Universal.

VIII—FRITZ OBERLIN

Aim of the Yarn.

To show that to serve Jesus Christ means doing the ordinary
work of life in the spirit of loving service to God and man.

Historical.

The work of Oberlin must be placed against the background of
the troublous period of the last days of the French monarchy and
of the Revolution. Fortunately, except for a short period during
the Reign of Terror, this upheaval in French history left this patch
of territory untouched. The principles of the Reformation entered
the valley via Strasbourg, and the first notable pastor was J. G.
Stuber, who preceded Oberlin in office from 1750 to 1756. The
scene of Oberlin's ministry was the Ban de la Roche (Valley of
Rocks), a fold of the Vosges Mountains in Alsace, near Strasbourg.
The valley was a most poverty-stricken region, and the few in-
habitants were so cut off from the rest of the world that they were
not merely ignorant and only half-civilised, but had a patois of
their own. The valley was named after the Chateau de la Roche
('ban'—a feudal lord's territory), a tenth century stronghold of
robber lords, which was captured by the Duke of Lorraine in 1469.
Orginally the valley had been the property of the Germans, but
in 1648 it passed to France, until in 1871 it was handed back to
Germany. In 1919, at the close of the World War, it became
French property once more.

Biographical.

John Frederick Oberlin (called 'Fritz') was born at Strasbourg
in August, 1740; son of a German professor in the gymnasium of
Strasbourg. He had a very hard upbringing, but the home was a
Christian one in the truest sense of the term. After attending the
school of his father for some years, Fritz went to the Protestant
University of Strasbourg, at that time one of the best in Europe,
where he studied a tremendous range of subjects, from languages,
science, mathematics, history and law, to theology. To pay for
this instruction, he worked as teacher of little boys. He became a
Doctor of Philosophy in 1763. He had always manifested a passion
for soldiering, and in 1767 had accepted a post as chaplain to a

French regiment, when J. G. Stuber, from the Ban de la Roche, looking round Strasbourg for a likely successor in his unenviable valley, urged Oberlin to accept this pastorate, and he was invested with this curé in April, 1767. From that day until his death in 1826, he devoted his life to his poor parishioners.

When the French Revolution caused anarchy and bloodshed everywhere, the very nature of Oberlin's ministry saved his life. For him Christianity was good citizenship, and as he cared little for the trappings of office, he laid aside his title and gown, and became Citizen Oberlin with few regrets.

IX—GEORGE WHITEFIELD

Aim of the Yarn.

To show how George Whitefield obeyed the call of God and carried the Good News of the Gospel to the degraded and neglected masses in England and America.

Historical.

England in the eighteenth century was in a parlous state from a religious and social point of view (see the notes on the Wesley Yarn*). Roads were bad, and many districts were quite out of touch with the capital. The north, of which we think to-day in terms of coal-fields and cotton and woollen industries, was entirely rural at the beginning of the century, though by the end of the period the Industrial Revolution was beginning. The upper classes were, for the most part, gross livers and atheists; the clergy were luxury-loving and lifeless as far as their pastoral duties went. The poor lived in unbelievable squalor and misery, and for the most part in complete ignorance. Crime was rampant, and fierce criminal laws which made the stealing of a loaf a capital crime, failed to deal with the situation. There was no effective police force; mobs rioted unchecked again and again.

'It was an age when reason was glorified as the highest of faculties and enthusiasm condemned as the worst of follies' (Somervell). A similar state of affairs in France ended, towards the close of the century, in the French Revolution. That no such terrible event occurred in England is largely due to the work of the evangelical reformers of the movement largely pioneered by George Whitefield and the Wesleys.

Biographical.

George Whitefield (born 1714, died 1770), was the son of a Gloucester innkeeper. He met the Wesleys at Oxford, and became an Anglican clergyman. He early acquired a great reputation as a preacher, and had a real genius in oratory. He was essentially

* In *Yarns on Christian Pioneers*.

a missioner, as we should put it, and did not settle long for any time. He joined the Wesleys in their mission to Georgia, and his special project there was the founding of an orphanage, in support of which a great deal of his subsequent preaching work was undertaken. His preaching influenced every rank of society, from members of the aristocracy (Lady Huntingdon was his chief patron) to the roughest and wildest miners. His methods were in several cases pioneer to the better-known work of John Wesley, *e.g.*, Whitefield first published journals, first founded schools, first undertook open-air preaching, and first summoned his preachers to conference.

Reference Books.

SOMERVELL'S *Short History of Our Religion* (Bell, 6s.); GREEN'S *Short History of the English People* (Macmillan, 8s. 6d.); *George Whitefield*, by A. D. BELDEN (from a library).

X—DAVID JONES

Aim of the Yarn.

To show how one man, with faith in God, is more than a match for an army of unbelievers.

Biographical.

David Jones was born in 1797, near Aberavon, Cardiganshire. He volunteered for missionary work in 1817, and was one of the two first missionaries sent out by the London Missionary Society to Madagascar. He arrived there in 1818, with a colleague and their wives and families, but within six weeks he was the sole survivor, and had to withdraw in a dying condition. In 1820 he returned, reached the capital (then Antananarivo, now Tananarive), and founded a mission there by winning the confidence of King Radama. After twelve years, helped by other missionaries, Christianity seemed firmly established. In 1828, on the death of Radama, Queen Ranavalona seized the throne. She was a strong-willed, obstinate woman determined to restore idolatry and the ancient customs. In 1836 the missionaries were forced to leave the island, but they had left behind a strong body of Christians, and the Malagasy Bible. Wave after wave of fierce persecution swept over the Malagasy Church, but failed to destroy it, and the number of Christians increased seven-fold during the persecution years. Several years after the death of Ranavalona in 1861, Ranavalona II burned the royal idols publicly and, following her example, thousands of the Malagasy flocked into the Church. Since 1864, five missionary societies have been at work in the island.

Reference Books.

David Jones, Madagascar Pioneer, by E. H. HAYES (in the *Pioneer Series*, R.E.P. 3s. net).

XI—FLORENCE NIGHTINGALE

Aim of the Yarn.

To show how Florence Nightingale's devotion to Jesus Christ and pity for the sufferer led her to become the pioneer of modern nursing.

Historical.

The background of Florence Nightingale's work is the Crimean War, which was begun in 1854 against Russia, by England, France and Turkey. The chief fighting was in the Crimea Peninsula, and the sick and wounded were sent across the Black Sea to Scutari, where a large barracks had been handed over to the English by the Turks for a hospital.

Nearly a hundred soldiers died every day in the place, and the preoccupation of the military authorities and the deadly restrictions of red-tape officialism made things worse. The appalling plight of the wounded after one great battle led William Howard Russell, a war correspondent, to appeal to English women, pointing out that the only female nurses at the war were the French Sisters of Mercy attached to the French Army. Women of all classes offered their services, but the military authorities and doctors were prejudiced. The need of the hour was a capable and determined leader and organizer. In the hour of extremity, the one woman in England who was qualified to lead—Florence Nightingale— stepped forward.

Biographical.

Florence Nightingale was born at Florence in May 1820, of wealthy and aristocratic English parents. From earliest days she evinced an interest in nursing, but her sense of vocation in this direction was sternly discouraged by her parents, for a nurse in those days was little better than a charwoman. But nothing would turn Florence from her purpose. There was no training to be had in England, so she had to go abroad and spend some months in training among the Catholic sisters in France. The outbreak of the Crimean War gave her her opportunity, and a sense that God had been leading and preparing her. She arrived at Scutari with thirty-four nurses on 5th November, 1854. From the outset, her work was hampered and harassed by medical jealousy and military prejudice, and at first she and her staff were only allowed to help the doctors. Difficulties that would have baffled a dozen ordinary women had to be faced, and were surmounted. Red tape was cut ruthlessly. The official statement 'It can't be done' was countered by an inflexible demand 'It must be done.' Only by an iron will, dauntless persistence, and first-class skill and efficiency, was Florence Nightingale able to take command of the situation, and get complete control. In the end, the elements of what we now call hospital organisation and equipment were set up at Scutari and the death-rate dropped from forty-two per cent on her arrival to two per cent. In spite of attacks of fever and broken health, she stuck to her post till the end of the war, and returned home a national heroine. She had no intention of taking such a rôle, however, and, evading all honours, used a fifty-thousand pound fund raised on her behalf for founding institutes for training nurses.

Although her never-robust health was permanently affected by her war-service, she devoted the rest of her life to developing plans for the uplift of the nursing profession, and the organising of the health service of an army in peace time. She was one of the founders of the Red Cross Society. She was the first woman to receive the Order of Merit, bestowed on her in 1907; she died in August, 1910, full of grace and honour and good works.

XII—MARY REED

Aim of the Yarn.

To show how for love of Jesus Christ Mary Reed devoted her life to the neglected lepers of India.

Biographical.

Mary Reed was born about 1854 in Lowell, Ohio (U.S.A.), was converted when about sixteen, and after some years of training as a teacher, volunteered for foreign mission work in connection with the Methodist Episcopal Church of America. She reached India in November, 1884, and was allocated to Cawnpore for work in the zenanas (women's quarters) of that city. After a few years her health gave way, and she went to Pithoragarh, in the Himalayas, for recuperation. Here she discovered a gathering of 500 lepers in a condition of absolute misery and hopelessness, the memory of which haunted her for years afterwards. She returned to Cawnpore and worked there for four years, until another breakdown in health sent her home to America. Doctors could make nothing of her mysterious malady until she herself identified it as leprosy. Instead of being appalled by the discovery, she saw in it the Divine purpose, and decided to devote herself to missionary work among the lepers in India.

In 1891 she volunteered for work under the Mission to Lepers in London, and went out to Chandag in the Himalayas to superintend their asylum there, where she laboured for fifty-two years. Her story, and her noble courage and devotion, captured the imagination of countless Christian people, and Mary Reed was confident that it was due to their prayers that her malady stayed, and that she was spared to live and work among lepers beyond the ordinary span of a healthy life. She died on 8th April, 1943, at the advanced age of eighty-nine, serving the lepers to the end, in spite of failing health and impaired eyesight an inspiration to all her colleagues. The key to her devoted life may perhaps be found in one of her early letters when she wrote: 'I am sure His love, His wisdom and His power are at work. Words are empty to tell of a love like His. He has enabled me to say, not with a *sigh* but with a *song*, "Thy will be done."'

For the story of how a cure for leprosy was at last discovered, see the Yarn on Isobel Kerr in *Yarns on Christian Torchbearers*.

Reference Book.

Mary Reed of Chandag (Mission to Lepers, 33, Henrietta Street, W.C.2. 9*d*., from whence latest information about this work can be secured.).

XIII—VERNON HAROLD STARR

Aim of the Yarn.

To show how a young man dedicated his life to following Jesus Christ in the service of the people of India, 'pledging everything' for Christ's sake.

Biographical.

Vernon Harold Starr (born 1882, died 1918), while apprenticed to a chemist at Oxford, came under the spell of Dr. Theodore Pennell, of Bannu, who believed that 'the finest thing in the world is the Medical Missionary.' Starr determined to follow Pennell,* and by dint of hard study won a scholarship in 1903, and entered King's College, London, to study medicine. In 1908 he took his degree in almost record time, a testimony to his enthusiasm and energy. In 1910 he sailed for India, and took up work at the C.M.S. Mission Hospital at Peshawar. He took charge of the hospital in 1914, and nearly wore himself out in its service as doctor and missionary. On 17th March, 1918, he was treacherously stabbed by unknown assassins, believed to be relatives of a boy converted by Starr, and afterwards killed by his family to wipe out the 'disgrace' of having become a Christian, and for whose death, according to Pathan custom, the doctor was held responsible.

Reference Book.

Vernon Harold Starr. A biography published by the Church Missionary Society (from a library).

* For the amazing story of Dr. Pennell's work see *Dr. Pennell: Afghan Pioneer*, by E. H. HAYES (R.E.P., 3*s*. net).

A LL R.E.P. BOOKS bear our colophon on the cover or title-page. It is a sign of practical help for the teacher on all phases of Religious Education, combined with high-grade production at a reasonable price, aimed to put our aids at the service of the widest possible circle of Teachers and Youth Leaders.

Send for full list of publications
(address on title-page)